Murder in the Mountains: The Muriel Baldridge Story

By Michael Crisp

Murder in the Mountains: The Muriel Baldridge Story
Copyright © 2011, 2012 by Michael Crisp

Cover design, book design and production by
R. Scott Hall

ISBN 978-1-4507-8226-5
Second Edition

Book Website www.kentuckycoldcases.com
Email: theveryworstthing@gmail.com

Give feedback on the book at:
theveryworstthing@gmail.com

Printed in the U.S.A

Contents

DEDICATION

This book is dedicated to the family of Muriel Baldridge. They are proud, strong people, and determined to keep Muriel's memory alive. I am honored to have played a small role in this endeavor.

- Michael Crisp

Foreword

Long retired from service and barricaded at both ends, the old rainbow arch bridge spanning the Big Sandy River between Prestonsburg and West Prestonsburg is nothing more than a relic now, a graceful but defunct architectural wonder from the past. It is the iconic image Floyd County has chosen to symbolize the pride and achievement of its citizens. But for some it will be forever linked to a time of pain and loss as well. It is the starting point for the tragic story of Muriel Baldridge, the beautiful teenage girl who was brutally murdered in 1949 and left on the riverbank in the shadow of the bridge.

Even now, more than 60 years after that terrible night, her senseless slaying and the confusing, disappointing efforts to bring her killer to justice is still current in the collective memory of Muriel's generation and a subject for discussion and speculation. But each personal recollection differs to some degree from the next and many details are either left vague or embellished according to the perspective of the person telling them. If Muriel's story is limited to oral history the emotional impact will survive but it will lose integrity and take on the characteristics of a myth in the same way that the bridge has lost its purpose and become a mere landmark. Not until this book has anyone attempted the painstaking research required to present an accurate overview of what happened to Muriel that night, the repercussions it had on the men accused of killing her, and the life-altering shock the community around her had to endure.

We may never know the truth about who killed Muriel but through this book we can learn the true facts surrounding the crime - a necessary step in understanding its place in local history and preserving the memory of Muriel. Her life was cut cruelly short; she never had the chance to write her own book or achieve anything out of her great potential. All we have left is her story and the least we can do to honor her is to tell it as well as we can instead of leaving it buried in newspaper archives or as the subject of skewed fiction in detective magazines.

For the few immediate family members who knew Muriel well and loved her deeply it is painful to revisit that time. They do not talk about it and it should not be mentioned to them. As Bede Jarrett wrote: "Sorrow you can hold, however desolating, if nobody speaks to you. If they speak, you break down." Their privacy must be respected. Still, in quiet conversations with me, a niece by marriage, they spoke about it one last time, believing that it is right for future generations to be able to share in the memory and the loss of Muriel. This book needed to be written and Michael Crisp has

handled it with compassion and insight. I am glad
to have been helpful in his search for information
about Muriel and grateful for the careful, skillful
way he has told a story so close to our hearts.

-Lynn Vance Preston

Chapter 1 - The City

Ernest Hemingway once said that "all things truly wicked start from an innocence", and for the families of Prestonsburg, Kentucky, in the summer of 1949, a single, wicked act left both a family and community grieving over the loss of not just one of its most beloved children, but also its innocence altogether.

The mysterious slaying of a popular young cheerleader, followed by a yearlong murder investigation that featured more twists and turns than the mountainous highways that wind their way throughout the outskirts of the city, seemed to leave many more questions than answers. Finally, after a sensational trial that left both the family and the community feeling both incomplete and heartbroken; it was clear that there would be no innocence left whatsoever. It was gone, and so too was Muriel Baldridge.

Nestled in the foothills of Appalachia, Prestonsburg is a small, eastern Kentucky town with a rich and storied past. The county seat of Floyd County, it was founded in 1797 and built along the banks of the Levisa Fork of the Big Sandy River, a tributary of the Ohio River that soon made the town a small hub of sorts for riverboat activity.

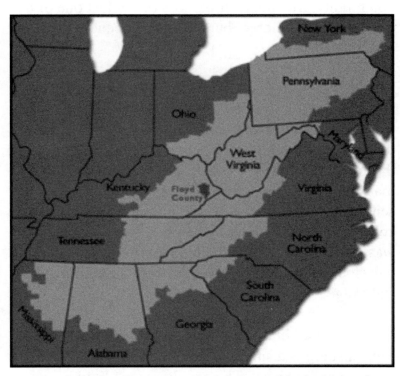

Floyd County, Kentucky, which is located in the heart of
Appalachia. *Courtesy of the U.S. Library of Congress*

Years later, Prestonsburg played a role in the Civil War, hosting 2 battles that took place within Floyd County: the Battle of Ivy Mountain and the Battle of Middle Creek. The Battle of Ivy Mountain took place in 1861, 10 miles south of Prestonsburg in the community of Ivel, and was a relatively small skirmish. The Battle of Middle Creek occurred the following year, and featured future U.S. president James Garfield leading a group of Union volunteers from Ohio as they virtually ended the presence of Confederates in the region.

As the 19th century gave way to the 20th century, coal mining became Prestonsburg's predominant economic industry, and the railroad replaced the riverboats as the primary means of getting to and from the city.

By the 1920s, the Chesapeake & Ohio Railroad Company had established itself as a significant part of the city's landscape. The C&O Railroad was a vital part of Prestonsburg's economy, and its depot station, located in an isolated neighborhood in West Prestonsburg on the west bank of the Big Sandy River, provided jobs to the local inhabitants as well as a steady stream of out-of-towners who patronized the local businesses. There was so much passenger and freight traffic at the depot that by 1925 it was decided that a bridge was needed to provide easier access between West Prestonsburg and Prestonsburg. In a partnership with Floyd County, the C&O Railroad commissioned a bridge to be built that would connect the two communities.

Built by the Steel and Lebby Contracting Company of Knoxville, Tennessee, the West Prestonsburg Bridge was completed by 1930. The bridge featured a unique "rainbow arch" design, and its originality made it a source of pride for the local inhabitants. At 400 feet in length and primarily constructed of concrete, the single-lane highway bridge was indeed a sight to behold - so much so that an almost identical bridge was built just 4 years later at Town Branch, a nearby community.

As the nation celebrated the end of World War II in 1945, Prestonsburg was no exception. Families were reunited as soldiers returned home, and Floyd County was enjoying a strong economy that hadn't been seen since before the Great Depression. It was a time to rejoice and celebrate not only a new era, but to celebrate hope, optimism, and a brighter future ahead.

The recently completed West Prestonsburg Bridge (the C&O Depot can be seen on the left of the photograph). *Courtesy of the Floyd County Historical Society*

Dedication of the West Prestonsburg Bridge in 1930 (Lon Moles, who would later be brought to trial for Muriel's murder, is the fifth man from the right). *Courtesy of the Floyd County Historical Society*

Chapter 2 - Muriel

Of the hundreds of students that attended Prestonsburg High School, Muriel Baldridge was one of its brightest stars. Blonde, pretty, and popular, Muriel (whose name was actually pronounced by family and friends as "Merle", which rhymed with "Pearl") was a cheerleader, well-known and well-liked by most everyone who knew her.

Muriel was the youngest of 7 children of Mr. and Mrs. George Baldridge. George was a section foreman for the C&O Railroad and worked just across the railroad tracks at the depot, while her mother, Bertha Hayes Baldridge, was a homemaker who spent most of her time caring for Muriel and her older siblings, brothers John (also known as J.R.), Bernard, and Dexter, and sisters Mary Hilary (who went by "Dee"), Irene, and Melda (who went by "Med").

The Baldridges moved to the house in 1942 when George was transferred to West Prestonsburg by the railroad company. It was a modest home, situated on a narrow strip of land in a small neighborhood, not far from the West Prestonsburg Bridge. Their backyard was overlooking the river, and the bridge was just over 200 feet away to the left of their home. Directly across from their front porch were the railroad tracks, and just across from the tracks was the depot station. At first glance, West Prestonsburg could have been mistaken for any quiet, sleepy little town, had it not been for the steady stream of noisy train traffic that stormed into the depot both day and night.

In the summer of 1949, Muriel was a senior at Prestonsburg High School, having just completed her junior year at the school. She was a precocious child, warm, generous and outgoing. Beautiful and friendly, she was popular amongst not only her classmates but also with practically everyone she knew. She was also a typical girl, and had the same interests that most any girl of her age would: dating, socializing with girlfriends, listening to music, attending church, and spending time with her family.

Muriel also possessed a quirky sense of humor. She would sometimes greet her dates at her front door in work boots. Her sister Irene recalled that Muriel did this with boys that she didn't actually want to date, in the hopes that this joke would "scare them off."

Muriel was still living at home, as the rest of her siblings were just starting to enter adulthood. Her brother Dexter had remained in Prestonsburg, working as a carpenter who often contracted with the Board of Education. J.R. worked for United Fuel, a gas company in nearby Warco, and Bernard had moved to Maytown after being appointed the Floyd County conservation officer.

Of Muriel's sisters, Dee had married Roland Burchett and Med had married Herbert Preston. Her other sister, Irene, married Willie "Red" Clark and was living just across the river, not far from the Baldridge home. Med had recently divorced Herbert Preston and had returned home to live at the Baldridge house, along with her 3 children, John, Sue and Wyn.

June had been a particularly warm month, with temperatures in Floyd County hovering around 90 degrees most days. By June 27th, the town's youth were excited about the traveling carnival that had arrived the day before. Muriel and her friends had talked that day about their plans for the night, discussing whether they would attend church, the carnival, or the softball game that was going to be played at the baseball field that evening.

Muriel's house was also buzzing with activity. That morning, she received a visit from her good friend, Donald D.L. "Dootney" Horn, a young man from the neighborhood whom she dated on occasion. "Dootney" told her that he was leaving town that afternoon for good, and he wanted to stop by and tell her goodbye.

Since Muriel's sister Med moved back home with her 3 young children, the house had once again become a hub of activity. But this was a particularly busy Monday because Muriel's aunt Mint was in town for the week, visiting from New Jersey and staying at the house. Mint was George's sister and one of the most beloved people in the Baldridge family. Muriel's

The Baldridge Home in the 1940s. *Courtesy of Lynn Preston*

other two sisters, Irene and Dee, had come over to see their Aunt Mint and had made plans to stay the night.

Before leaving the house, Muriel took a bath at 5 p.m., and then according to her sister Med, she "lolled about the house" until 6 p.m., when she accompanied her aunt to the railroad depot across the street from her house. Muriel borrowed a beautiful blue sun dress to wear for the evening. After seeing Muriel in the dress, her Aunt Mint gave her a string of pearls to wear as well, remarking on how the necklace would be a perfect matching accessory to the dress.

Muriel's friend Sybil McKenzie arrived at her house to walk with her into town. "Save me some watermelon," said Muriel to her sister Med before the two young girls left the house that evening.

The 1948 squad (top) and the 1949 squad (bottom). *Courtesy of Barbara (Bolen) Porter*

Muriel Baldridge, her sister Melda, her sister Irene, an
unidentified aunt, and her sister Mary Hilary ("Dee") (L to R).
Courtesy of Tish Clark and Ruthie Burchett Gray.

Chapter 3 - A Grim Discovery

Everything came crashing down however on the morning of June 28, 1949, when at 5:30 a.m. a city bus driver named Tom Calhoun was driving across the West Prestonsburg bridge. Seeing something unusual in the bushes below the bridge, he parked his bus nearby at the depot station, then ran across the tracks, shouting for one of the employees at the station to call the police. To Calhoun, it appeared as if someone had either jumped or fallen off the bridge and landed on the riverbank below.

A local bread truck driver named Don Pitts was, along with his brother, making his usual Tuesday morning delivery run to nearby David, Kentucky. Pitts also saw something that looked unusual on the riverbank just below the bridge. He parked his truck and began making his descent toward the object. As Pitts approached within a few yards of the object, he realized it wasn't an object at all - it was a person; a young girl in a blue sun-back dress, lying motionless in the grass. Her face and skin were pale, her hair was bloodied, and she had several wounds on her head. Although it was very apparent the girl was dead, Pitts quickly ascended the riverbank, waving his arms frantically and shouting for help as he scurried back up the hillside to the neighborhood above.

By the time the authorities arrived, a small gathering of onlookers were at the scene. A few men

George Baldridge and his granddaughter, Sue Preston, on the front porch of the Baldridge home. *Courtesy of the Louisville Courier Journal*

This is believed to be the last picture of Muriel Baldridge (Pictured left, on her her front porch with a family member). *Courtesy of Lynn Preston*

from the small, tight-knit neighborhood community approached the body and began to speculate on the identity of the body.

Behind the matted hair was Muriel Baldridge, the 17-year old daughter of Mr. and Mrs. George Baldridge. In the most heartbreaking of ironies, Muriel and her parents lived just two hundred feet up the riverbank from where she was lying.

Some of the people gathered near the body left the scene to begin spreading the news about the grisly discovery. Others remained, lifting the girl's body out of the bushes and carrying her to the top of the riverbank.

Sheriff Troy Sturgill arrived soon after, and began to examine the crime scene while trying to keep the throng of curious onlookers at bay. Arriving separately was Floyd County Coroner Brady Shepard. Shepard briefly examined Muriel's body, sent for an ambulance, and asked the ambulance driver to send her body to the Carter-Callihan Funeral Home. Muriel's parents, George and Bertha Baldridge, had not yet emerged from their house, and Shepard felt it would be best for her parents to identify her at the funeral home rather than on the grassy riverbank, surrounded by curious onlookers.

The ambulance made its way back across the bridge, passing cheerleader Sybil MacKenzie, who had just heard that a young girl had been found murdered underneath the bridge. Sure that it was Muriel, she was running as fast as she could down the bridge and towards Muriel's house. One of Muriel's brothers, Dexter Baldridge, arrived soon after with his wife Eileen. Two of Muriel's sisters, "Med" and Irene, joined them on the front porch, where Muriel's father George was standing silently, absorbing the tragic news about his youngest daughter. Sybil stormed onto the porch and began begging George to tell her where Muriel was, but he remained silent. A few minutes later, the family went inside to deliver the heartbreaking news to Muriel's mother Bertha.

As Muriel's family gathered inside the home to comfort each other, two of the men from the throng that had gathered on the riverbank decided that, rather than have George identify his daughter's body, that the task should be done by Muriel's best friend, Joan Hall. Joan was still in bed when she heard the men arrive, speaking urgently with her mother on their front porch. Joan's mother then came into her bedroom and shared the terrible news with her, and asked that her daughter go with her to the funeral home to identify the body.

Just 15 years old, Joan was extremely scared as she was led into the funeral home by her mother. On the mortician's slab was a body covered by a white sheet that was peppered with bloodstains. As the sheet was removed, Joan saw Muriel lying motionless on the table - still clad in her sun dress, with her face swollen,

16

Floyd County Sheriff Troy Sturgill (left). *Courtesy of the Floyd County Historical Society*

Joan Hall (right), a friend of Muriel's who helped identify Muriel's body. *Courtesy of Barbara (Bolen) Porter*

Joan Hall (pictured right), seated with Ruthie Mayo (left). *Courtesy of Barbara (Bolen) Porter*

and her hair matted and bloodied. Joan glanced down at Muriel's hands, noticing the tiger-eye ring on her little finger, as well as scratches on her delicate hands, and dirt under her fingernails. Joan looked over toward Grady Shepard, telling him that the body was indeed Muriel's.

While performing the autopsy, Shepard noticed that Muriel "had sustained five skull fractures, any one of which could have caused death." He further elaborated, saying that "the fractures were clean cuts and could have been made by a tire tool or a brick."

Muriel and her friends. Front row (left to right) Ruth Hall, Sue Goble, and Berdella Hall. Back row (left to right) Muriel Baldridge, Doris Ann Clark, Joan Hall, Ruthie Mayo, and Sharon Bradley.
Courtesy of Mary Ann James and Emily James Anderson

Her dress had been torn, most likely in a violent struggle. It also appeared that the girl had been dead just a few hours.

Attorney James Evans surveys the crime scene. The "X" represents where police believe Muriel was beaten, and the dotted line shows where she was dragged, ending at the location where Evans is seen standing. *Courtesy of the Louisville Courier Journal*

Shepard also worked closely with the detectives investigating the crime scene itself. "The slayer had apparently attempted to throw his victim into the swift river," said Shepard, who could clearly see a long path, approximately 50 feet in length, among the dirt and

Attorney James Evans holds the uprooted peach tree that was found at the crime scene. *Courtesy of the Louisville Courier Journal*

grass of the riverbank that appeared to have been made by Muriel's body as it was being dragged to the river below. Her killer's intent was to drag Muriel down the bank and throw her into the rushing waters of the Big Sandy River, but while fighting for her life she struggled mightily with him while being pulled down toward the waiting waters. A pool of blood was also found beneath the bridge at the base of a concrete pier. This was several feet from her body, suggesting that Muriel had been initially attacked here, then later dragged down the riverbank towards the water. Apparently his exhaustion from the struggle, coupled with the rough piles of debris that had washed upon the riverbank, made the last 10 feet of the journey impossible for him, and he was unable to complete his task to push her into the river. After pulling her through a small corn patch, he left her just 10 feet from the water's edge.

Not far from Muriel was an uprooted peach tree which revealed yet another sign of the deadly struggle she had with her attacker. Shepard found a string of pearls - presumably Muriel's - dangling from one of the tree's branches, which he carefully removed from the tree and placed in the front pocket of his shirt. It was presumed that this necklace was Muriel's, and that it had fallen off while she was being dragged down the riverbank. "The peach tree was as big around as your arm", said Woodrow Burchett, the charismatic Floyd County Attorney, at a Tuesday afternoon press conference that took place at his office. Reporters frantically took notes during Burchett's press conference, asking the occasional question amidst a large crowd of onlookers that had hastily gathered inside the courthouse.

Police found an 8-inch lead pipe near Muriel's body that appeared to be blood-stained, but Burchett was unsure if this pipe was indeed the murder weapon. "The value of the clue," he said, "must await laboratory tests." Shepard however didn't believe that the pipe was the murder weapon, insisting that although her skull had been crushed during the attack,

Woodrow Burchett, Floyd County Attorney *Courtesy of the Floyd County Times*

"Muriel's wounds were very clean and did not look as though they had been made by a pipe."

He believed that the murder weapon was an object more akin to a brick or a tire iron, and that in all likelihood it would never be found; the killer probably threw it into the river after beating Muriel to death with it.

As reporters jockeyed for position in the crowded office, Burchett went on to add that "the ground surrounding the body revealed that a terrific struggle had taken place", referring to the uprooted peach tree and a trail of loosened soil that stretched for several feet down the riverbank, eventually ending near Muriel's body. He went on to add that "other evidence indicated that the girl had been seized on the bridge and dragged down the steep embankment to the spot where she was found," but he didn't elaborate on the specifics of that evidence, nor did he give reporters an idea of what led investigators to that theory.

Thanks to the moist dirt that encompassed most of the riverbank, the investigators were able to find numerous footprints in and around the area where Muriel was found. After examining the footprints, Shepard said that they were made by "about an eight or nine shoe." The trail of footprints indicated that after leaving Muriel's body beside the river, the killer "ran up the hill between the house occupied by the girl's parents and the house occupied by the name of

Dotson." The houses were located a few hundred feet apart, and there was no indication if he was trying to go toward one of the houses in particular. It was also noted that the footprints "disappeared into some gravel in the alley."

When questioned by reporters about the search for possible suspects in the case, Burchett confirmed that there was no doubt that Muriel "met her death at the hands of an unknown person", and that "several suspects were being investigated", refusing to give out any names or information or offer any additional speculation, other than the fact that "no one has been formally booked."

As the press conference drew to a close, a collective sigh of relief could be audibly heard throughout the room when Burchett announced that, after Shepard's examination of her body, it was concluded that Muriel had not been "criminally (sexually) assaulted".

As Tuesday night drew to a close, a crowd of townspeople had gathered outside the courthouse. Although peaceful and nonviolent, a sense of anger and urgency was in the air as the people of Prestonsburg were anxiously awaiting answers - and anxiously awaiting justice for the young girl who lost her life the night before.

Chapter 4 - A Night to Forget

Details from the night of the murder began to emerge. Muriel had been in the company of 3 of her friends, Thelma Hollingsworth and Sybil MacKenzie, both of whom were from Prestonsburg, and Gail Hamilton, who lived in nearby Emma. The 3 girls were also Muriel's classmates at Prestonsburg High School, and Sybil was also a member of Muriel's cheerleading squad. That evening the 4 of them attended a softball game at a nearby playground, watched a movie at a local theatre, and then decided to attend a traveling carnival that was set up in the city's Porter Addition.

"The four of us met in front of the drugstore after the movies Monday night and decided to go to the carnival," said Hollingsworth to reporters from the Louisville Courier Journal. "We got to the carnival about 9 and didn't stay more than an hour. Muriel wanted us to go home with her and have some watermelon, but I couldn't because I had to do the dishes. We wanted her to come downtown with us and get a ride home, but she said she wasn't afraid to walk the bridge - she had done so many times."

Hollingsworth said that Muriel didn't mention having a date or any other plans that evening, and that they didn't encounter anyone unusual during the night. "On the way to the carnival, one of the younger boys in school hit Muriel with a toy pistol," added

Hollingsworth, "and she told him to stop it because he already had done it once before, but that's all that happened."

After leaving the carnival, Muriel and her friends made their way home, walking the streets of Prestonsburg in the dark, humid night. At approximately 10:15 p.m., Muriel and her friends came to the corner of 7th Street and the Mayo Trail and stopped for a moment; they were near Muriel's house, which was across the river and just a short walk across the bridge.

According to Brady Shepard, the coroner who was also pulling double-duty as a spokesman for the investigation, "the girls offered to walk across the bridge with Muriel but she laughed and said she had crossed it alone 'hundreds of times'". It would be the last time that they would ever see Muriel alive again.

Some neighbors living near the bridge reported hearing screaming that evening. The closest house to the bridge on its western side belonged to Mr. E.S. Dotson and Mrs. Maggie Dotson. Mrs. Dotson distinctly remembered the time as being 10:20pm when she heard screams coming from outside her home. She had gone to bed for the night and awakened by a scream. "While I was getting to the back door, there were several other screams," she said. "The last scream was when I turned on the light and opened the door. I didn't hear anything after that, and

I hear so many noises around the bridge that I went back to bed."

Sue Goble, a fellow high school cheerleader and friend of Muriel's, also heard screaming that night. She was visiting her friend Betty Lou Tackett at the home of Betty Lou's mother, Mrs. James Dotson. Mrs. James Dotson lived just across the aqueduct from the E.S. Dotson's home, and according to Sue, she and her friend "got a stack of funny books and made some sandwiches. We laid there and read for a long time."

The two girls reported hearing screams coming from outside the house that evening. "We heard this scream and then sat up in bed," Sue said. "Then this woman spoke. I thought she said 'Hey, where are you going?' but Betty thought she said 'Hey, where did you go?' I thought maybe a girl was walking across the bridge and some man tried to grab her. She said 'that's my grandmother' after she spoke, but I didn't recognize the voice. Immediately after the scream a motorcycle went by."

Sue also thought that the cries she heard were coming from the nearby Prestonsburg General Hospital, thinking that it was probably a patient that was arriving there. Sue said that the screams frightened her, prompting her and Betty Lou to turn off all of their bedroom lights.

"Later we heard all these trees rustling," Sue added. "We first thought it was rain, but then it stopped. I said 'Betty, rain doesn't stop and start like that'. Betty has a tree there and we thought maybe it was somebody trying to climb up in the tree. We heard

Thelma Hollingsworth, one of the three girls who were with Muriel on the night of the murder. *Courtesy of the Louisville Courier Journal*

this lumbering. I said it's under the bridge and Betty said 'no, that's in my back yard.' Then after we had quieted down, we turned the light back on, read some more funny books and went to sleep."

Some speculated that Muriel's killer also intended to rape her, but her harrowing cries, which were followed by the porch lights coming on in the neighborhood to investigate the screams, made the killer flee before he could complete his task.

Mrs. Elbert S. Dotson (left) and her granddaughter Betty Lou Tackett (right). *Courtesy of the Louisville Courier Journal*

"I don't think anyone could get mad at Muriel," said fellow cheerleader and close friend Sybil MacKenzie. "All the boys would give their eye teeth to be seen with her. She was always so cheerful to be with, always laughing and smiling. She never got mad."

"She only went out with high school boys here or in towns near here," shared Clyde Neal George, a 19 year-old recent graduate of Prestonsburg High School.

Sue Goble, a friend of Muriel's who heard screaming on the night of her murder. *Courtesy of Barbara (Bolen) Porter*

Clyde Neal George *Courtesy of Barbara (Bolen) Porter*

"I figure it was some person who knew she went home that way and was watching for her, or someone who had been drinking."

It was rumored that Muriel had a date planned that evening with a young man from Paintsville named "Slick" Melvin. According to investigators, Melvin's parents were "considered to have money" and he was a "lone and spoiled son." It was established that Muriel had been recently seen in his company, however the exact date of that meeting could not be determined.

"She didn't talk to anyone at the carnival except the ticket man who gave me passes the year before," added MacKenzie. "It seems every time we went to a carnival something bad happened to Muriel. The last time Muriel went to a carnival she caught pneumonia and was sick for months."

Muriel's mother, nearly inconsolable during her interview with police, said that she "wasn't alarmed" when Muriel hadn't come home that evening, believing that she "thought Muriel was staying with a friend overnight."

Muriel's father George was also trying to help investigators by providing what little information he knew about what could have happened. "I don't think it was any of her high school boyfriends," he said, "but whoever did it should be hung right there on the bridge where she was murdered."

Clyde Neal George (top left) posing with the Prestonsburg
High School's yearbook staff. Also pictured are two of
Muriel's good friends, Ruthie Mayo (front row, center) and
Joan Hall (bottom right). Joan was the girl who identified
Muriel's body. *Courtesy of Barbara (Bolen) Porter*

Chapter 5 - Suspects

The investigation into who killed Muriel Baldridge was in full swing, and Sheriff Troy Sturgill began compiling a list of suspects, the first of whom was Richard Funk. Funk, an 18-year old hitchhiker originally from Carlton, Michigan, was arrested an hour north of Prestonsburg in Catlettsburg, Kentucky. He was brought to a police station in Catlettsburg by a truck driver named Oscar Miller, who was currently living in Clove, Ohio, but was a former resident of Prestonsburg. Miller offered the young hitchhiker a ride after hearing about the slaying in Prestonsburg earlier that day, and during their trip Miller began to grow suspicious of Funk's behavior, disheveled clothing, and muddy shoes.

At the police station, Funk told police he had "been visiting friends near Prestonsburg" on the day of the murder, but had "left town about 2:30pm." Funk remained in police custody for several more days before being released.

After bringing in several suspects for questioning, most all of whom were soon released, Sheriff Sturgill arrested Junior Osborne "for questioning in connection with the death of Muriel Baldridge." Sturgill described the youth as a "rejected suitor of the girl". At the time, speculation was running rampant that Muriel's murderer was likely a boyfriend, as it was reported that she "was very popular in the town's teenage circles, with numerous boyfriends but no one in particular." Burchett and Sturgill questioned several of Muriel's male friends, including Paul Martin, a student at Prestonsburg High School who had been dating Muriel frequently over the past year. Several of Muriel's male friends were questioned during the early part of the investigation, but there were no strong leads.

By now, the Federal Bureau of Investigation and Kentucky State Police had joined in the hunt to find the killer, and approximately 30 local men "joined in a posse to aid the Sheriff". Sturgill even deputized approximately 70 local men in order to assist in the investigation. The local government also retained the nationally-famous Pinkerton Detective Agency to help with the search for the killer. With so many people and agencies working on solving the crime, one unidentified local man was quoted as saying that "there have been too many fingers in the pie, and everyone now fancies himself a private eye."

Muriel's body was prepared at the Carter-Callihan Funeral Home, and Mrs. May Martin, operator of a beauty parlor in Prestonsburg, cleaned Muriel's hands, face, and hair prior to her being laid in her casket. Muriel's funeral service took place at 2 p.m. on Thursday, June 30th, at the Irene Cole Memorial Baptist Church in Prestonsburg. It was officiated by the Reverend L.D. Benedict, and had an estimated attendance of 3,500 people - considerably more than Prestonsburg's population of 2,300 at the time. During Muriel's service, the rest of the city was silent, as all of the stores and businesses had closed. Cars lined the streets, and hundreds of people were gathered inside and outside of the small, brick church.

"It took more than 30 minutes for the still-stunned townspeople to shuffle by her white-and-gold casket in the church," wrote Louisville Courier Journal reporter Eve Mark. "The body was gowned in orchid and white. On the casket were pink and red roses and gladiolas."

Picture of the Prestonsburg High School Football Team, including cheerleaders (front row, left to right) Doris Ann Clark, Ruthie Mayo, and Muriel Baldridge. *Courtesy of Mary Ann James and Emily James Anderson*

Gerald Leslie, teacher at Prestonsburg High School. *Courtesy of Barbara (Bolen) Porter*

Muriel's 1949 junior class picture. Muriel is in the front row, seated fourth from the left. Directly behind her is teacher Gerald Leslie, who considered Muriel one of his favorite students. *Courtesy of Barbara (Bolen) Porter*

The church's altar was virtually unseen, as it had been blocked by a wall of flowers that had been delivered to the church. There were 75 floral arrangements that were delivered by Prestonsburg's only florist shop - which represented the entire inventory of flowers in the store.

Members of the Prestonsburg High School football team carried Muriel's casket into the church at 2 p.m. The 5 remaining members of Muriel's cheerleading squad were also in attendance. Muriel's father and mother sat in the front of the church, flanked by their six children.

As the choir began to sing, almost everyone in the church was overcome with emotion. For the service, Reverend Benedict chose the 25th Chapter of Matthew, reading aloud "And the Kingdom of Heaven is likened to 10 virgins." He declared that Muriel was one of the 10 virgins, and that "out of this tragic experience, the people of Prestonsburg would gain a greater understanding of life and how to live it."

Hundreds filed past Muriel's casket to bid her goodbye, including Mrs. Woodrow Burchett, who was also Muriel's Sunday school teacher at the church. "It seems I always could teach Sunday school so much better when Muriel was here," shared Mrs. Burchett, who stepped out of the line to share her feelings with Revered Benedict. "She was so good for the class."

One of her high school teachers, Gerald Leslie, also remarked "School won't be so nice without Muriel."

After leaving the church, the townspeople stood outside, with the silence broken only by the occasional conversation about whether Muriel's killer would ever be caught. "Do you suppose he's here to see her?" asked a man in the crowd, speculating that the murderer may have attended the funeral.

The funeral procession began, as hundreds of cars made their way down First Avenue toward a private cemetery on the outskirts of Floyd County.

Chapter 6 - The Investigation

After Muriel's funeral, the investigation into her murder intensified. Calling the slaying "the most fiendish crime that's ever happened in this county", Coroner Brady Shepard was steadfastly determined to see her killer brought to justice.

Joining the team of law enforcement officials investigating the murder was Arch Thompson, a detective with the Kentucky State Police, and J.E. Combs, a Kentucky State Trooper from the nearby Pikeville detachment. Thompson, who resided just north of Prestonsburg in Louisa, released a statement speculating that "while no motive had been officially established, I am inclined to believe that jealousy was behind the killing." Thompson wasn't alone in thinking that Muriel met her death at the hands of a rejected suitor, and discounted the idea that she had been attacked purely with the intention of rape.

Thompson was a tall, heavy-set man with a very commanding presence. He had recently become one of the state's first detectives when the Kentucky State Police was formed in the summer of 1948, when Governor Earle Clements enacted legislation to create the organization. Until then, Kentucky's only statewide law enforcement agency was the Kentucky Highway Patrol, a 40-man force whose primary responsibility was to enforce speeding laws on the state's highways.

Kentucky Governor Earle Clements. *Courtesy of the Floyd County Historical Society*

It was a scene that had never been seen before in the small city of Prestonsburg, as State, County and City police had converged to investigate a crime. Hours later, the Federal Bureau of Investigation sent an agent to Prestonsburg, who told reporters that he was "there just to lend a hand if needed." With the agent's arrival, gossip began to spread that the suspect might actually be a fugitive that was wanted by the F.B.I.

Some of the investigators began to quietly speculate that the killer was most likely a local man, or men, because Muriel had been carried from the bridge down a somewhat hidden, narrow path, and only someone familiar with the riverbank would be able to expertly navigate it in the darkness of night. Authorities went on to speculate that the killer "either had a long acquaintance with the terrain or had studied it in a premeditated plan for murder."

As Trooper Combs continued to interview Muriel's friends at the high school, law enforcement officials were still trying to maintain some semblance of control at the crime scene. Large crowds of "curiosity seekers and amateur detectives" were trampling the ground and hampering the investigation, and a Tuesday morning rainfall made matters worse. Fortunately, Dr. Earl T. Arnett, a Prestonsburg dentist, was brought to the crime scene to make several plaster of paris casts of the footprints that were found near Muriel's body, footprints that the detectives were certain belonged to the murderer.

One of the first orders of business for Detective Thompson was to release Richard Funk, the 18-year old hitchhiker brought in for questioning a day earlier. "We don't have much reason to think he's the man who killed the girl", stated Thompson, "he doesn't fit into the case." After a routine check with Michigan police, he was released after being booked on a vagrancy charge.

In nearby Paintsville, investigators thought they had a break in the case when a man named "Damron" claimed to have seen a young girl being beaten near the river on the night of the murder. Thompson rushed to the police department in Pikeville to question Damron, an attention-seeking drunkard who admitted that he had been drinking all evening and was in nearby Allen that evening, several miles from the murder site.

A jury room was set aside to conduct most of the questioning, and over 50 people had been brought in for interrogation during the first 3 days of the investigation.

The Floyd County Times continued to run stories about the investigation, and other area newspapers, such as The Paintsville Herald, diligently covered the story as well. "This is what we have been reading about so long and now it's happened here," said some local residents in Prestonsburg in an article for The Paintsville Herald. "Our killings have always been clean, nothing brutal like this. Who could have killed this innocent girl?"

The newspapers also received passionate pleas from their readerships to find Muriel's killer. The Paintsville Herald published this heartfelt letter to their editor from a concerned citizen:

"When, and if, the brutal slayer of young Muriel Baldridge is found and brought to trial, will a Floyd county jury again accept the old, farcical plea of self-defense?

That is a question which, on the face of it, is nonsensical, but which in fact is no more silly than the criminal-petting gullible juries which for all these years now have been turning loose upon society, with little or no punishment, a long array of killers.

This girl who died at the hand of a soulless wretch was young and lovely. She was harming nobody. She had by only a few years left the fairyland of childhood, barely had entered on young womanhood. Dark strata, gems and thoughts of murder were far from her mind. Yet she was the one to die, to be dragged away from the scene of her death as if by a werewolf.

Can justification be found for this crime? We wonder. If the killer is of an influential, wealthy family; if he has an appealing personality; if his story is pitiful enough…we wonder.

Self-defense? It is time Floyd County's people act in self-defense. This is not the time for rash individuals, or men who dote on violence, to talk of taking the law into their own hands.The law has been in their hands, all these years, and they have done little with it.

In our horrified realization of the fact that it not only can happen here but actually has, our deep indignation should be turned upon ourselves, not against any one individual or any one official. Self-excoriation and examination are the ingredients of the treatment we need.

Let us face this particular crime as we should face all crime - as good citizens of courage, coldly bent on seeing that justice prevails, nothing short of justice.

For others will die and other crimes will be committed. This present sorrow of ours is but a part of the dark panorama of crime we have been gazing upon and shall continue to face, with eyes half-closed, until the remaining forces of right in Floyd County get ready to fight for the right."

- The Paintsville Herald, June 30, 1949

Chapter 7 - A Blank Wall

Just a week after Muriel's murder, the lack of new leads prompted Sheriff Troy Sturgill to ask for assistance from the community in solving the case. Sturgill released the following statement to the media on July 7th:

"If you have information vital to efforts of authorities to solve the mystery surrounding the murder of Muriel Baldridge, and wish to keep your identity concealed, your wishes will be granted, and yet you will be paid $500 for your help if your information leads to the arrest of the killer."

Sturgill asked for anyone who had information about the slaying to mail a letter to the Sheriff's Post Office Box with the information, and that the identities of those who sent the letters would remain in the "strictest confidence." The investigation hadn't yielded any new leads over the last week, prompting the front page of the July 7th Floyd County Times to report that the frustrated investigators were "facing a blank wall".

Desperate for answers, detectives and county officers were trying anything to generate new information about the case, including questioning witnesses under the effects of "truth serum". On the evening of Wednesday, July 6th, detectives questioned 5 people who allowed themselves to be administered the drug. Hopes ran high that the truth serum, which was administered by prominent psychiatrist Dr. J.H. Rompf of Lexington, Kentucky, would illicit a confession from one of the persons being questioned.

Excitement was in the air as word spread throughout the city that "truth serum" was going to be used in the investigation. The "closed door" interrogations took place inside the Sheriff's office, however the fact that those being questioned would be under the influence of "truth serum" was an "open secret." The courtyard outside the Sheriff's office quickly filled with local townspeople, all of whom were gathered beneath an open window in order to hear the proceedings. Several of the people gathered in the courtyard said that those being interrogated responded very loudly to investigator's questions, giving responses while speaking in a slow, slurring manner that sounded as if they were drunk. By night's end, all 5 of the witnesses maintained their innocence and failed to share any information about other potential suspects that could help investigators.

One of the five people being questioned under the influence of the drug was Elbert K. Dotson, better known at E.K. Dotson, a former taxi cab operator and current restaurant owner. Dotson's home was in West Prestonsburg, very near the riverbank and just a few hundred feet away from the Baldridge home. In recent years, Dotson, who was 45 and described as very quiet and introverted, had done a great deal of work on his home. In the basement of his home was a "bath house" that he operated, which would allow coal miners that arrived at the Depot station a place to get themselves clean after arriving in town. More recently, he had built a restaurant on the top level of his house in order to accommodate miners as well. Dotson's father, Elbert S. Dotson, better known as E.S. Dotson, owned a home in the neighborhood as well, close to both the river and the bridge. It was E.S. Dotson's wife Maggie Dotson that was one of the witnesses who reported hearing screaming on the night of the murder.

As the truth serum interrogations drew to a close, detectives had quietly eliminated the possibility that the suspect could be someone from the area. When word got out that some in the area suspected a missing man who had worked at a local filling station up until the morning of the discovery of Muriel's body, police issued a "two-state alarm" for Kentucky and West Virginia so he could be located and brought back to Prestonsburg for questioning.

Upon hearing that he was wanted for questioning in the investigation, Sammy Moore of nearby Tomahawk, Kentucky, telephoned Chief of Police Bill Blackburn and offered to come to the police station for questioning. Moore had indeed quit his job at a local filling station on the morning that Muriel's body was discovered, and became a person of interest in the investigation when his wife told officers that she saw him Tuesday evening and he was acting nervously and told her he was "in trouble." It was speculated by police that Moore's nervousness was caused by the fact that he was wanted on a cold check charge.

As the questioning of potential suspects began to subside, investigators began re-examining the physical evidence that had been collected at the crime scene, looking for meaning in these clues. Other items were also rumored to have been found at the scene. Some said that a quarter had been found at the scene near Muriel's body, and that the coin may have fallen from her purse, which was also missing. "I understand the girl's beads were found in a bush, a few feet from the bridge," said State Detective Arch Thompson. "To this day I have not seen these and if any other detective has, I don't know of it."

Making matters even worse was the fact that some rumors within the police department were making the rounds that all of the physical evidence in the case that was recovered at the crime scene was missing, including the 8-inch pipe that many believed was the murder weapon.

Even with the assistance of the Pinkerton detectives, who were being privately funded by a handful of local citizens, the case had reached somewhat of an impasse. By week's end, the money set aside to fund the private detectives had been exhausted, and the Pinkerton Detective Agency departed from Prestonsburg. "All we know is that a murder has been committed here," said the detective before leaving. "There are 191 rumors and 190 of them are wrong."

State Detective Arch Thompson turned over the information he was gathering on the case to the Pinkerton detectives, as well as State Detective Walter Woods, a new investigator who was brought in from Manchester, Kentucky. "Feeling is running high in the case," commented Woods, "and I'm trying to get my bearings and to learn what has been done so far. If this case doesn't crack within 48 hours, it may be quite a while before we have a solution."

Thompson was also quick to let the public know just how extensive the investigation had become. "We are working with the Pinkerton Agency, the Chesapeake & Ohio detectives, Floyd County Sheriff Troy Sturgill, and his whole darn department."

Despite the challenges facing the investigators, Thompson remained committed to finding Muriel's killer. "I am not quitting the case," he said. "Even if they send John Edgar Hoover here on this murder. I will never quit the case until it's solved."

State Police Detectives Arch Thompson (bottom row, third from left) and Walter Woods (bottom row, fourth from left).
Courtesy of the Kentucky State Police

Chapter 8 - A Ride Home

Muriel's case had not only captured the attention of the community, but also the nation. Newspapers across the country were covering developments in the investigation, and on July 12th, a Kentucky singer/songwriter named Nora E. Carpenter penned a sorrowful ballad about the case that she recorded soon thereafter:

The Death of Muriel Baldridge
by Nora E. Carpenter

Have you heard the sad, sad story?
It happened in the month of June,
Muriel Baldridge met with tragedy;
While in her youth and bloom.

Oh how lonely and sad without her,
Yes, we miss her more and more;
some sweet day we'll go and meet her,
On that bright celestial shore.

She was a high school cheerleader,
Her age was about seventeen;
She met her death by fatal blows,
As was proved upon the scene.

A horrible crime to be committed,
Soon t'will be brought to light;
Her many friends and relations,
Still pressing, pressing hard the fight.

Oh parents we know the grief is great,
So sad so sad we can't forget;
The cruel wretch who killed your child,
His life should pay the debt.

Alas his case is left with God,
To guide his wretched soul;
If he does not confess on earth,
At the judgment t'will be told.

Pray on pray on comrades of Muriel,
Oh Father and Mother if living,
You can't see Muriel here anymore,
Just meet her up in heaven.

For two weeks the investigation continued, with police having several "persons of interest" but no official suspects. That all changed on Tuesday, July 12th, just two weeks after Muriel's murder, when it was reported that Donald L. "Dootney" Horn, a 21-year old neighbor of Muriel Baldridge, was being brought in for questioning.

Deputy Sheriff Harold Conn swore out the warrant against Horn soon after Horn, who was currently in El Paso, Texas, told the El Paso police department that he was "wanted for questioning" in the Baldridge murder case. The Governor of Kentucky, Earl C. Clements, then issued a requisition for Horn's extradition back to Kentucky - dispatching State Detective Walter Woods by plane to El Paso to retrieve the fugitive. "He's the logical suspect," said Woods, just prior to boarding his plane bound for El Paso. "The state would not go to the expense of returning him were authorities not certain he was the murderer."

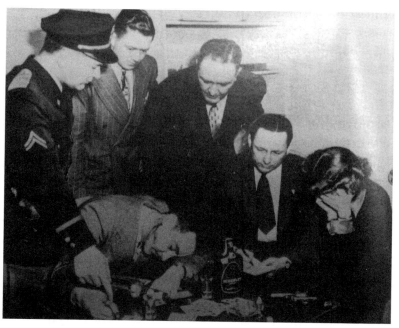

State Detective Walter Woods (second from right), seen here participating in a police training exercise *Courtesy of the Kentucky State Police*

As word quickly spread throughout the community that Horn was a possible suspect in the slaying, there was a prevailing feeling among those who knew him back in Prestonsburg that doubted he could have anything to do with Muriel's slaying. Known as a "friendly boy" with no previous history of a police record, Horn lived just a block away from Muriel Baldridge in their West Prestonsburg neighborhood. His father operated a coal truck company in Prestonsburg, and "Dootney" dabbled briefly in the coal business before leaving for El Paso with the intent of opening a furniture business. Others who knew Horn speculated that he had simply tired of Texas and was parlaying Muriel's murder investigation into getting a "free ride home" back to Kentucky.

The police gathered a great deal of background on Horn by speaking with one of his closest friends, John Archer Campbell. Campbell, who went by the nickname "Burhead" because of his curly blonde hair, had planned to leave with Horn to depart for Texas and Mexico on Monday, June 27th. He said that Horn was attempting to purchase a 1929 Ford from a local man, E.K. Dotson, for a "$35 down payment and the rest when he catches up with me."

At noon on Monday, Campbell met Horn and realized that the"car deal fell through." He said that Horn told him to "pack a small bag and bring a blanket," stating that they would "ride as far as possible and would camp by the roadside at night 'hobo fashion.'"

The men had agreed to meet later that day at Bingham's Grocery Store at 3 p.m., however Horn didn't show up for the meeting. Campbell "passed it off as one of Donald's many eccentricities," believing that Horn might have actually decided at the last minute to accompany a female friend, Beverly Shepherd, to Georgia.

Campbell told investigators that he didn't think Horn had ever dated Muriel, believing that she would never have dated any of the young men that were from "the Bottom," which is what the West Prestonsburg neighborhood was known as throughout the area. He also believed that Horn didn't kill Muriel, because he wasn't "the vicious or mean type."

Muriel's sister Med recalled that Horn had stopped by the house on the day of the murder. Wearing blue trousers, rolled up to his calves and sporting a cigar in his mouth, Horn came by to tell Muriel of his plans to move south.

Horn was brought back to Kentucky on Wednesday, July 13th and housed in a Paintsville, Kentucky jail. Upon his return to Kentucky, he was able to produce a piece of evidence that exonerated him of any wrongdoing. He had left for El Paso by bus on the evening of Muriel's murder, Monday, June

27th, departing from Mt. Sterling, Kentucky en route to Memphis, Tennessee. The ticket stub he retained proved that the bus he departed on left Mt. Sterling at 6:04 p.m. that evening, approximately 4 hours prior to Muriel's murder.

Horn produced the ticket stub to investigators on Wednesday, July 13th, but spent 3 days in the Paintsville jail while local law enforcement checked out his story and verified the authenticity of the ticket stub. After concluding that he was no way involved in the murder, he was released from jail on Saturday, July 16th. "Why was I held from Wednesday till Saturday, is what I want to know," grumbled Horn after his release.

"I knew Muriel very well but had nothing to do with her killing" he added. "I guess it looked funny because I left town the same day." He also said that he hoped to soon return to El Paso to start his furniture business.

Chapter 9 - Bill Gamble

While the public was immersed in questions about Muriel's murder, State Detective Arch Thompson was searching for answers. After focusing for several days on local suspects, he shifted his attentions to the people who were working at the carnival on the evening of the murder. Many in the community thought the carnival was a logical choice for the killer. The traveling carnivals of the south had a somewhat seedy reputation for employing "questionable characters", migrating strangers who could easily commit such a crime with the hopes of vanishing into the night air, and into the next city.

Thompson and Sturgill began talking to the employees of Bee's Shows, the company that owned the carnival. They spoke to employees who had been working that evening, but most everyone had an alibi. They needed a break - and that break came on Thursday, July 21st, when a 15-year old carnival worker named Olen Collins named former carnival worker William "Bill" Gamble as the slayer.

Sheriff Sturgill, accompanied by Deputy Sheriff Harold Conn and Special C&O Railroad Agent G.L. Gray, made the short trip to the neighboring Perry County Jail to interview Collins, the young carnival worker who had been brought in for questioning in the case. Collins told Sturgill that not only had Gamble, an acquaintance of Collins and former employee of the carnival, had killed Muriel Baldridge, but that he was there when it happened. Gamble, a 24-year old originally from the small community of Red Fox in Knott County, denied any involvement with the murder.

Collins, a Kentuckian from nearby Magoffin County, said that he was riding in a car driven by Gamble on the night of the slaying, and that as they crossed the West Prestonsburg Bridge, they saw Muriel crossing it by herself. Collins said that Gamble "snatched" her into the car on the Prestonsburg side of the bridge, "clapped his hand over her mouth, circled and drove back across the bridge and up the Middle Creek road a distance of about 3 miles."

Collins went on to add that Gamble "took the girl into a field" while Collins waited in the car, and both Gamble and the girl returned about 30 minutes later. "And when they came back she was crying, and he acted like he was mad."

"She was looking at him and crying," Collins said, "and he picked up a screwdriver, it was a big screwdriver, about 14 inches,; he picked the screwdriver off the floor and hit her on the head with it.

As the detectives listened intently, Collins continued with his story. "She didn't cry. She just fell with her head back on the front seat." Collins went on to say that after Gamble struck Muriel and she fell unconscious, he "drove back to the bridge and parked on the left side, over by the weeds."

"Then he took the girl by the arm and pulled her out of the car and got her under his right arm and dragged her under the bridge." Collins went on to add that Gamble took the screwdriver with him while he was dragging Muriel down the riverbank, and when he returned to the car alone, he put the screwdriver under the front seat. Collins said that he noticed blood on the screwdriver, as well as blood on Gamble's trousers. With Collins in tow, Gamble began driving back towards Prestonsburg.

When asked about the whereabouts of the trousers, Collins said that Gamble "burned them just this side of Virginia," and offered to take officers to the spot where he watched Gamble burn them.

The authenticity of Collin's story was further bolstered by the fact that 6 separate witnesses had recently reported seeing a "big man and a little man" on the bridge that evening around the time of the murder. At 6 foot 3 inches, Gamble was considerably taller than his youthful companion, and investigators were certain that the pair would be positively identified once they were brought before the witnesses.

Gamble, who sported an "extensive criminal record", had been jailed earlier in the week in Perry

William Gamble, former carnival worker accused of Muriel's murder. *Courtesy of the Pittsburgh Post-Gazette, Pittsburgh, Pennsylvania*

County for questioning in the case. According to Deputy Sheriff Conn, Gamble was also being questioned "in connection with the disappearance of a husband and wife while they were en route north from a visit to Florida." The couple hadn't been heard from in two months, and Conn believed that the car Gamble was driving belonged to the missing couple. Gamble maintained that he had recently purchased the automobile.

Fearing a potential "mob scene", Detective Arch Thompson secretly moved Gamble to a jail in nearby Hazard, Kentucky. Soon after, police brought Collins to the jail and confronted Gamble in his cell to officially identify him as the killer.

Although Collins' statements about the night of the murder easily provided the best lead of the month-long investigation, his story was not without its questions: How could Gamble restrain Muriel and drive one-handed through Prestonsburg at the same time? Why would he bring her back to a largely populated area to kill her and dispose of her body?

Investigators were also concerned that Collins, towards the end of his questioning, became nervous and confused. It seemed that some portions of his answers seemed contrived and slightly contradictory. In any case, it appeared that the Muriel Baldridge murder case had been solved, and that plans for a trial would be soon underway.

Olen Collins (right) points out William Gamble (left) at an unidentified jail in Kentucky as special C&O Railroad agent G.L. Gray (center) observes. *Courtesy of the Floyd County Times.*

Chapter 10 - Just Guessin'

The collective hopes of an entire city came crashing down on Wednesday, August 3rd, when 15-year old Olen Collins recanted the eyewitness account he gave investigators the week before.

"I just told a lie," confessed Collins. "I don't know a thing about the death of the girl."

Collins said that he first heard about the murder from his mother, who contacted him while he was traveling from Abingdon, Virginia to his home in Duco (Magoffin County), Kentucky. He said that he fabricated the story he told in his original statement to police. "I was just lyin'," said Collins, "I just guessed about it."

When asked by officers how he knew certain facts about the crime, such as specific locations in and around the crime scene, and that the victim screamed during her attack, he said that he "was just guessin'."

Authorities were still not convinced that Collins was telling the truth. After his initial statements identifying Gamble as the killer, Collins told investigators that he "felt better", and that he "hadn't been able to sleep or think about anything else." If he was lying now about what he saw that evening, what were his motives? He was also unable to verify his whereabouts on the night of the murder, or give police the names of any specific people that either saw him or conversed with him that evening.

Adding to the curiosity was that Collins had refused to submit to a lie detector during his initial statement, even though he had steadfastly maintained that Gamble had committed the murder. He had now changed his mind about the lie detector, saying "it's all right with me if my mother agrees." He told authorities that he first refused the test "because I was afraid the courthouse roof would blow up."

Despite Collins' heartbreaking revisions of his story, investigators did get some good news when another witness came forward to shed some light on the case. Investigators had heard that an African-American carnival worker named George Burton "Shorty" Williams had been riding with Collins and Gamble on the night of the murder, so Williams was brought in from London, Kentucky, to talk to police. It was soon discovered that Williams' car ride with the pair took place on the Saturday after the murder, which was corroborated with an official from the carnival.

After a thorough investigation of Gamble's car, which had been taken to Detroit for analysis, County Attorney Woodrow Burchett announced that there were no bloodstains in the automobile. He also added that the screwdriver believed to possibly be the murder weapon was not in the vehicle.

The mood of the community was best described by The Floyd County Times, reporting that the murder investigation had been "thrown back to its demoralizing beginning, with the murder overcast in mystery and dangled in a skein of lies, rumors and false leads."

Chapter 11 - A Fresh Start

A few weeks later, the investigation into the murder of Muriel Baldridge took yet another bizarre turn on Saturday, August 20th, when William "Bill" Gamble, the former carnival worker who had been accused of the crime by Olen Collins, confessed to the murder. Signing a written confession at a police department in Cincinnati, Ohio, Gamble provided a shocking twist to the mystery that had captivated the community throughout the summer. Most everyone felt that it was sure to bring some much-needed closure to everyone who had been demanding justice for Muriel.

Content with the confession, Sheriff Troy Sturgill remained somewhat unsettled. He felt strongly that Gamble may not have acted alone, suspecting that two other carnival workers may have had a hand in Muriel's murder. When questioning Thomas Howell and "Whitey" Cochran, both men told Sturgill the same story that Gamble had told him about his whereabouts on the evening of the murder.

Howell and Cochran maintained that Gamble was with them when they left Greenup County, Kentucky on the afternoon of Monday, June 27th. When they arrived in Perry County, Gamble took the automobile, stranding the two men with no means of transportation.

Sturgill knew their story was a lie. He had been working with Perry County Deputy Sheriff Elmer Holliday, who had testimony from another officer, a coal miner, and Gamble's relatives that verified Howell and Cochran had arrived in Grapevine, Kentucky (Perry County), in the early morning of Tuesday, June 28th. Upon arriving in Grapevine, the two men told a handful of people that they had ridden with Gamble, and that their overnight journey took them from "Greenup via Route 7, from Grayson through Sandy Hook, to West Liberty, Salyersville, Prestonsburg and Hindman."

Sturgill's investigation found that Gamble, Cochran and Howell met up on June 20th in Springfield, Kentucky, and arrived on June 26th in Greenup, Kentucky. The next day, Monday, June 27th, they helped set up the carnival in Prestonsburg. While working, Howell expressed his intention of returning home to Detroit, Michigan, and Gamble and Cochran asked if they could go to Detroit as well.

Gamble, Cochran and Howell had each tried to persuade investigators that they had left for Detroit on the afternoon of June 27th, several hours prior to Muriel's murder, however police had discovered that their journey north actually began on Tuesday, June 28th.

Cochran and Howell's whereabouts on the night of Muriel's murder were rendered almost moot when

the news came that Gamble had signed a written
confession at Cincinnati's police headquarters. The
first part of the confession was a general description of
the events during the evening of the murder:

> "On Monday, June 27, I got in the car at
> Grapevine along about 9 or 10 o'clock at
> night. I left the boys over there. They
> sent me after some whiskey. That is
> what they sent me after. I never got no
> whiskey. I never came back. I picked up
> the boy over by Estill. We went down
> there where the girl was killed -
> Prestonsburg.
>
> We went across the bridge there and the
> girl was standing there and we stopped.
> We asked if she wanted a ride and she
> says no. We got out and tried to put her
> in the car anyhow, see. This boy Olen
> Collins had a hold of her and I hit her.
> We put her in the car and drove up to the
> depot and turned and went back to the
> bridge and left her there. When I left her
> I went back and got in the car and drove
> off. We went to Virginia then."

The second part of the confession was in
'Question and Answer' form:

Q: Your name is Bill Gamble?

A: Yes.

Q: Did you pick up Olen Collins at Estill, Ky., on Monday, June 27?

A: Yes, sir.

Q: Did you, with Olen Collins, drive to the carnival at Prestonsburg, Ky., on Monday night, June 27?

A: Yes, sir.

Q: Where did you go when you left the carnival on that night?

A: We went back down there to that bridge.

Q: Did you drive across the bridge to the West Prestonsburg side and turn your car and drive back to the Prestonsburg side?

A: Yes, sir.

Q: Did you get hold of Muriel Baldridge on your way back across the bridge from West Prestonsburg to Prestonsburg?

A: Yes.

Q: Did you seize the girl by her dress before you got out of your car?

A: No.

Q: Did Olen Collins help you get Muriel Baldridge in the car?

A: Yes.

Q: Did you drive your car out in front of a filling station after having placed Muriel Baldridge in the car and drove up Middle Creek Road?

A: No.

Q: Where was the first place you hit Muriel Baldridge?

A: When I first picked her up.

Q: Was she in or out of the car when you hit her?

A: She was out of the car.

Q: Where did you hit her the next time?

A: I hit her in the car the next time.

Q: Where was the car?

A: At the depot.

Q: Where did you next hit her?

A: When I got her out of the car over at the bridge.

Q: Where did you next hit her?

A: I didn't hit her no more.

Q: Did you strike Muriel Baldridge with a screwdriver under the bridge?

A: No sir.

Q: Bill, do you mean to say that you didn't drive this girl up the Middle Creek Road?

A: I never.

Q: Didn't you drive your car up Middle Creek and then back the car over into a side road surrounded by a corn field?

A: No, sir.

Q: What did you do with the screwdriver, Bill?

A: It is in the car. It was when I last saw it.

Q: Who was with you besides the Collins boy?

A: Nobody.

Q: What clothes were you wearing at that time?

A: A pair of blue pants and a blue shirt.

Q: Had you and Olen figured on picking up some girl?

A: No, sir.

Q: Were you in the car when you first caught the girl?

A: No, sir.

Q: Were you on the bridge?

A: Right there, at the east Prestonsburg side.

Q: If you were out of the car, were you hid on the bridge?

A: No, sir.

Q: How did you catch her then?

A: We got out of the car. She was standing there.

Q: Bill, where did you leave the Collins boy?

A: I left him in the Abingdon, Virginia, jail."

While Gamble was confessing to Muriel's murder, 15-year old Olen Collins was also brought to Cincinnati, whereupon he decided to change his story yet again and name Gamble as Muriel's killer. In his own handwriting, Collins penned a 12-page statement describing the events of the evening, a portion of which was released for publication:

"He reached out a window of the automobile and grabbed the girl after seeing her on the left side of the bridge. The girl started screaming. Gamble got out and slapped a hand over her mouth, then pushed her into the car on the driver's side. Her head struck the steering wheel real hard and her head fell over the back of the seat. She was quiet for a while and then started screaming again. Gamble held a hand over her mouth and drove with one hand. Near an underpass he nearly ran against a girder and he released her and she started screaming again.

I was in the back seat. After this he told me to drive. I climbed into the front seat, Gamble was in the middle with the girl pushed over on the right side. Gamble kept a hand over her mouth. He directed me out a country road and ordered me back into a wagon trail. I told him I couldn't back up. He then backed the car out and I took the back seat again.

The girl was crying and Gamble told her to shut up. He took her from the car into a cornfield and stayed about 20 minutes. The girl was still crying when they returned to the car. We started back toward Prestonsburg. Gamble reached on the floor and got the screwdriver and struck the girl twice when she continued screaming. But she was quiet after that.

When we reached town he dragged her from the car. She was limp and couldn't walk. Her feet were dragging behind her. Gamble dragged her under the bridge and then came back to the car and drove away. He warned me to say nothing. Outside the town he stopped and took off his pants and shirt and made me hand him others. He then got some sticks, a 5-gallon can of gasoline and started a fire and burned up his clothes. He kicked the ashes around and we drove away."

The following day, on Sunday, August 21st, a Cincinnati Enquirer newspaper writer named Paul Lugannani reported that while interviewing Gamble, he told Lugannani that his confession was untrue. Gamble told the reporter that he had signed the confession under duress from the police, and that he didn't even know how to read or write.

Gamble claimed that he made the confession because the acting Cincinnati detective chief, Captain Patrick Hayes, threatened to kill him. "Bill Gamble was as calm as we are right now when he made that statement," said Sheriff Sturgill. "There were no threats and he made that statement under his own free will, but I can understand a fellow like him coming up with something like this," Sturgill added. Besides, I don't believe he's afraid of anybody or anything."

Both Gamble and Collins remained in custody and were returned "to an undisclosed jail" in Kentucky. "Gamble wouldn't last 5 minutes in Prestonsburg," said Sturgill. "The people are too incensed over this crime." Howell and Cochran, the carnival workers who were still under suspicion for obstructing justice in the investigation, also remained in custody, under guard at a secret location. Meanwhile, Prestonsburg city officials passed legislation banning future carnivals within the city limits, in the hopes that it would help prevent any incidents like Muriel's murder from happening in the future.

Chapter 12 - Leo Justice

Just when it appeared the case would offer nothing new, word soon came that Leo Justice, a 23-year old member of a prominent family in nearby Pike County, had confessed to Muriel's murder. "Another fool like me trying to get his neck broke," said Bill Gamble, who had recently signed - and later recanted - his own confession to the murder.

Strangely enough, Justice made his confession on Friday, August 26th, saying that he killed the young cheerleader with a tire tool, and like Gamble, repudiated the confession the following day. Justice's initial statement of confession read:

> "I hereby make a truthful statement
> about what I know about the Death of the
> Baldridge girl at Prestonsburg.
>
> I met Collins and Gamble at the Shelby
> Junction while hitchhiking to Pikeville.
>
> I came to Prestonsburg with the boys and
> we picked up the girl. I hit her with a
> tire tool to keep her quiet, but I didn't
> know she was dead."

Justice was brought from Pikeville to Prestonsburg immediately following his confession, and was taken by investigators to the bridge. He took the investigators 2 miles west of the city to Abbott Mountain, where he said Gamble took Muriel "down an embankment and was gone about three-quarters of an hour."

It was now clear that the Baldridge case was "the most perplexing murder ever to confound officers and detectives in this section of Kentucky," according to the Floyd County Times. With "two confessions, repudiations, a re-confession on the part of Gamble, a statement by Olen Collins accusing Gamble, another Collins statement claiming he knew nothing of the murder, then a third statement putting the finger on Gamble", the people of Prestonsburg wondered if this mystery would ever be solved.

Making matters even more confusing was the news that Olen Collins had reverted back to his statement that he had no knowledge of the crime. This news, coupled with the release of carnival workers Thomas Howell and "Whitey" Cochran from police custody, was even more disheartening to the citizens of Prestonsburg.

Also looming was the fact that the grand jury would be convening on Monday, September 5th, and authorities were unsure who they would indict. Sheriff Sturgill openly insisted that the grand jury would be asked to indict 15-year old Olen Collins.

"The boy, regardless of his guilt or innocence of murder, is too dangerous to turn loose on society," remarked Sturgill. "He has committed perjury and obstructed justice. Regardless of pleas made for him, it is nothing but right that he be brought to trial."

Whether Justice would also be indicted remained to be seen. Despite denying his statement the following day, Justice's murder confession prompted authorities to keep him in custody. He spent the weekend in the nearby Pike County jail before being moved to an undisclosed location on Tuesday, August 30th. Even though he was vocal in maintaining his innocence of the crime, law enforcement officials said that Justice "shrank" while being driven across the West Prestonsburg Bridge en route to jail, becoming "highly nervous" especially on the west end of the bridge near where Muriel's body was found.

It was said that Justice initially confessed after being arrested at a Pike County hotel on a drunk charge, telling Pike County Sheriff D.C. Moore "I hope I don't go to the electric chair for it, but I probably deserve it." He later revised his story to Moore however, claiming that he had been drunk for the last 3 days prior to his arrest and that he had no part in the girl's murder. "I don't know anything about it," said Justice to Pike County Sheriff D.C. Moore. "I don't remember anything I told you. It all seems like a dream."

"You have dreamed yourself into a lot of trouble," responded County Attorney Pierce Keesee.

Chapter 13 - Untouchable

In the days that passed, State Detective Arch Thompson had quietly withdrawn from the case, choosing instead to focus on other investigations and separate himself from the frustrations involved with the mystery of Muriel's death. Whereas many in the community wondered if William "Bill" Gamble, Leo Justice, or any of the numerous other people that had been investigated over the summer were guilty, Thompson adamantly felt differently.

"The real murderer, in my opinion, hasn't been caught," Thompson shared, "he hasn't even been touched." Thompson's September 6th statement echoed a sentiment that was growing throughout the community, as the investigation into Muriel's murder was back to square one.

Sheriff Troy Sturgill, already threatening to bring Olen Collins before the grand jury, was also entertaining the idea of bringing Gamble before it as well. Sturgill opted instead to postpone his appearance before the grand jury in order to focus on a new lead that had materialized in the case. Sturgill didn't divulge any information about the new lead, remarking only that it was "something hot."

Speculation grew that the new lead was a witness who would be coming forward soon to say that he either witnessed the murder or saw a man at the murder scene at the time that the screaming was heard that evening. This new lead was provided by Detective Beck of the Pinkerton Detective Agency, who had quietly re-entered the investigation when additional funding had been procured from some local benefactors.

Thompson was very leery of anything in Beck's investigation being either helpful or valid. "The Pinkertons haven't got a thing on this case except the material clues that have passed from hand to hand," Thompson said. "The way the case stands, it is blocked and no one has a chance to move it. When the Sheriff, the state and the FBI don't move a case, it just can't be moved. Entirely too much interference! The way this case is being muddled at present, I wouldn't become involved at any cost."

Thompson was being repeatedly encouraged by his superiors to return to the investigation, but repeatedly refused - insisting that he wouldn't personally return to the case until "the private eyes, the curiosity crews, and publicity seekers quit messing things up and the good citizens quit throwing their money away".

"This doesn't mean," Thompson added, "that I have forgotten or dropped the case. I would appreciate an opportunity to work on it, unhampered."

Sheriff Sturgill had still been working tirelessly on the case, and he was looking forward to the chance to bring one or more of the suspects before the grand jury. He reiterated his desire to indict 15-year old Olen Collins for perjury and obstruction of justice, but also mulled bringing an indictment against Leo Justice, the Pike County man who had recently confessed and then recanted his confession. But Sturgill respected the opinion of Pike County Sheriff D.C. Moore, who firmly believed that Justice was not Muriel's killer, making an indictment against Justice unlikely for the time being.

Local law enforcement officials were also given some new information that they hoped would be helpful in the investigation. A state police report was made public that a young couple in Ashland, Kentucky was the victim of an in-home invasion, and authorities believed the two men that broke into the home had a possible connection to Muriel's murder.

The men broke into the home of Mr. and Mrs. Glenn Bartley, threatening Mrs. Bartley, who was alone at the time. Mrs. Bartley said that the two men, one of whom was an older gentleman with several teeth missing and the other was a young man, were both intoxicated. She told police that they grabbed her wrist, took her to a bedroom, and made her sit quietly there while they went through the house, threatening to do "something worse" to her if she didn't remain quiet.

She went on to say that the men had flashlights, looked through her house, and later left in a half-ton truck.

During the investigation into the home invasion, Mrs. Bartley's uncle told police that he believed the two men had been in the neighborhood working on sewing machines, and that a cousin of his overheard the men saying that they "had better lay out for six or more weeks." The cousin also heard the two men mention the Baldridge murder during the same conversation.

Meanwhile, back in Prestonsburg, the grand jury met and decided not to indict anyone in the Baldridge murder case. The grand jury would soon reconvene on September 29th, with Sheriff Sturgill still convinced that "Bill" Gamble was guilty of Muriel's murder.

Chapter 14 - A Plea for Action

The community of Prestonsburg was still searching for answers, and still hungry for justice. With the September 29th grand jury deadline looming, many in Prestonsburg felt compelled to ask for help in solving the case.

One of Muriel's peers, a teenage girl who was a classmate of Muriel's at Prestonsburg High School, wrote an anonymous letter that was published in The Floyd County Times:

"To the People of Floyd County:

For more than two months now, I have been waiting this opportunity. Now, I have decided to speak.

On June 27th, a pretty teen-age girl was killed by the hand of some unknown person or persons. Many things have been done about it but, somehow, it hasn't been enough. Those closely connected with the crime have fallen just a little short of what they should have done. Many good, honest citizens have been sincerely concerned with the solution, yet it has been unsatisfactory. It all started at the very beginning, and up until right now, there have been many blunders. People find themselves thinking that just a little more should have been done.

Although as long as this town continues to exist, people will try to give their opinion. I want to have myself put on record as saying this: With everything having been done, I still think it isn't enough. Perhaps you will say, "Well, this person asks too much," but I don't. The solution of this thing is more than just a murderer being brought to justice. To me, it means two very important things: I knew Muriel, and she was one of the nicest people I have ever known. For that reason alone, I think we haven't done enough. Because of this alone, I could say these things, but there is one more thing that I think gives me every right to speak my piece. That is this fact: as a girl Muriel's age, I'd like to think it was safe for me to go out at night without fear that the same thing might happen to me. I think of the grief of the girl's parents, and pray that my parents might never have to suffer the same things. I'd like to know that the people of Floyd County cared enough about its youth to take care of it, and protect it, that it might grow up to lead successful lives in the towns of our county. What good is it to spend hours at graduation telling us about the successful lives we should lead, if we are afraid to go out, even with friends, remembering what has happened to one of us, and fearing for our own lives?

This is more than just another murder. It is a thing that the community as a whole should take upon itself to solve. Now don't get me wrong! I don't mean everybody should turn amateur-sleuth, or that each man should take it upon himself to punish the murderer, but I mean this: Every mother and father should, because of their own children, make it a point to see that every chance is taken, and every clue examined until they know it backwards, and upside down. Every boy who has a sister should be willing to help, for no matter how they get along, no man would like to have that happen to his sister. Every girl should give her right arm, if only their lives are in safety again, instead of unsure danger.

If the people of Floyd County don't get after the "right" people, and get them back to work doing things that should have been done, they will never again have the security that they have loved in their homes. When the committer of such a crime can be allowed to run loose, and evidence is found and not given to the proper authorities until days later, then I think I, with the rest of my gang, are going to lead a pretty miserable life in Prestonsburg. One of the things we cherished so much is the freedom we can have. That, above all, made the town mean more to us. Many times I have walked across the bridge at night with friends, and never thought a thing about it, but now, I won't even walk up the street a little way, for fear that I might run face to face with our murderer, and become just another "crime" in the courthouse records. Unless someone gets to work, that is exactly what is going to happen.

Crime is not new to this county, but never before has it been so brutal, and so seemingly useless. Even if it was a "carnival worker," should we allow those kind of men to walk around, and know that if they are slick enough, they won't get caught? I don't know who murdered my friend. I don't even have any ideas. All I know is this - how many young girls find themselves dreaming at night of just such a thing as this happening to them? How many people lock their doors at night, where they used to be open, and safe? How much less is the fun for everyone? Any one who has spent the summer here has noticed that whenever this case is mentioned a deadly gloom falls over the crowd.

Perhaps some people are stupid enough to think that if we just sit tight and save the taxpayers' money, the criminal will just walk in one summer night and say, "Well - I did it - hang me!" Mind you again - I'm not trying to run the Sheriff's office for him - I'm just saying that it would be better to spend some of that money, and make this place happy and safe again than to shirk a duty and make us unhappy.

In the name of the teen-agers of this good county - I ask this: If you, the people of Floyd County, and the officers of it, let us down, we will never again live the happy, carefree lives we have been accustomed to in the past. We will not be able to do this ourselves as we take our positions in the community, for then it will be too late. Finally, I ask that something more be done, so that, if this thing is never solved, we will at least be able to hold our heads up and say we did our best. All we ask is a little more effort, a little harder trying. We are helpless, for our opinions are not yet ready to be heard as a reliable source. If wishing would help, it never would have happened. So in the name of all that is decent and right, let's have something done so that at least the right people work together, and we won't ever have to worry about these kinds of things again. I ask this for myself, for Muriel, for our parents and loved ones, for you and for all generations of teen-agers to come that they might not have this fear we must have, until something is definite or final. We are helpless, so as the bosses of this county - I beg of you - that we all will live happier, healthier lives, unmarred by the death of another of our girls, or tainted by the utter worthlessness or uselessness of us to handle a thing that was a national concern. We have always said we were the best county, so we must prove it not by idleness, but by diligence, so all can breathe easier, and our friends can sleep better knowing that Muriel's death has at last been avenged.

Please, for yourselves, do something!

A TEEN-AGER"

The community was growing ever doubtful that the case would be solved, and several challenges still lie ahead. Funding for the Pinkerton Detective Agency had ran out, and Detective Beck left soon thereafter. Muriel's parents also made an impassioned plea to State Detective Arch Thompson for him to return to the case, but it did no good.

Despite the growing discontent in the community, the Sheriff's office diligently continued to seek answers in the murder investigation, and the idea of setting up a reward fund began to take shape. The Floyd County Times was instrumental in turning the idea into reality, which led its longtime editor and publisher, Norman Allen, to publish a front-page plea to the citizens of Prestonsburg, challenging them to help find Muriel's murderer by contributing to the fund.

Money Talks - and May Cause Somebody to Talk About a Murder

The Times, like many others, is not convinced that a solution has been reached in the murder of Muriel Baldridge, but until now when it appears that an indictment may be made with the tangled skein of mystery so filled with the inexplicable that an innocent man may be convicted or a guilty man may escape the full penalty he should pay, this newspaper has refrained from urging any steps other than those taken in the ordinary course of investigation.

At this late date, fearful that the full story of this horrifying crime may never be known, we give Page One prominence to a plea for a reward fund.

We have our own check ready as a starter. We ask all who believe that every vestige of doubt should be removed, if humanly possible, before some defendant is held guilty of a crime he did not commit, or declared innocent of one which he did commit, to join us.

Money talks; and it will cause somebody who knows to talk. If it doesn't, whatever amount you subscribe will be refunded to you. If it does, the fact that you contributed to the solution of a baffling mystery and helped to avenge the death of an innocent girl should be sufficient reward.

Let us not make it necessary that relatives of the slain girl contribute to raise this fund. They have suffered enough from bereavement and heartbreaking suspense. This county and its people together can afford at least $2,000 or $3,000 to pay for information to establish the guilt of a fiendish killer who, if permitted to escape just punishment, will, one day, repeat his bloody crime.

This suggestion is not made with any idea of interfering with any officer or group now, or at any time, working on this case. It is not made with the idea of saying Bill Gamble or Leo Justice or any other man is guilty or saying who is innocent.

It is made because the investigation is far short of a satisfactory ending. Our check for $100 is ready. Is yours, in any amount?

Make all contributions to the Muriel Baldridge Reward Fund and hand or mail them to The First National Bank, Prestonsburg, Ky."

- *The Floyd County Times, Summer, 1949*

A reward fund was soon started to find and convict Muriel's murderer. Contributions poured in from the local community. Along with the $100 pledge from The Floyd County Times, other contributors included the Prestonsburg Fraternal Order of Eagles, who pledged $500 to the fund. Other local men such as John S. Hampton and N.M. White, Jr. followed suit. It was kept at the First National Bank of Prestonsburg, and administered by bank cashier Russell. H. Hagewood.

Norman Allen, Editor and Publisher of the Floyd County Times. *Courtesy of the Floyd County Historical Society*

Chapter 15 - Summer's End

On September 29th, a very busy grand jury convened, hearing not only evidence in the Baldridge murder case but also several other cases that were brought before it. In all, 239 witnesses were heard during the session, including two other local murder cases.

Fortunately for "Bill" Gamble, he was spared an indictment for murder in Muriel's case, and Olen Collins was also the recipient of good news: he too was spared the indictment that Sheriff Sturgill had sought for obstruction of justice. In somewhat of a surprise, Leo Justice instead was the only person indicted in Muriel's murder case, but rather than murder it was for the obstruction of justice charge that Sturgill had initially sought for Collins. While Justice had been released from jail on a $500 bond, it was discussed during the hearings that authorities would seek a juvenile hearing in the near future for Collins, with the aim of having him committed to a reform school.

It had been just over 3 months since Muriel's murder, and as summer drew to a close, it was looking as if her killer would never be caught.

It was now January, and nearly 4 months had elapsed since there was any news about the case. Behind the scenes, State Detective Arch Thompson had quietly rejoined the investigation, re-teaming with newly-elected Chief of Police Epp Lafferty and newly-elected Sheriff Banner Meade. Suddenly, new life was breathed into the search for Muriel's slayer, as investigators announced that two new clues had materialized: a pair of stained trousers and a pillow.

Lafferty didn't say who the trousers belonged to, or who he and the rest of the investigators believed they belonged to, but he said that the pants appeared to have bloodstains on them. The pillow also had a blonde hair on it, which was the color of Muriel's hair. The trousers and pillow, along with the clothing that Muriel was wearing on the night of the murder, were currently in the possession of the Federal Bureau of Investigation. "It's my opinion that the items are connected with the death of the girl," said Lafferty. For the first time in months it was believed that the killer would be caught.

Lafferty, who had previously served as a deputy when Sheriff Troy Sturgill was in office, was a popular fixture in Prestonsburg. He had spent most of his lifetime in law enforcement, which began at age 16 when he was deputized by the Sheriff's department and just a few weeks later shot a man to death during a police standoff. Known for his no-nonsense style, as well as his penchant for carrying his pearl-handled, .38 caliber Smith and Wesson pistol on his hip holster as he walked the city's streets, Lafferty had the confidence of most everyone in the community that he would bring Muriel's killer to justice.

Coincidentally, word had recently come from Perry County that William "Bill" Gamble, long considered the primary suspect in the murder case, had been reported missing from jail. He was being held in Hazard at the Perry County jail, but had apparently escaped on December 3rd with a fellow inmate, Buster Fugate. Fugate was from nearby Hindman and was serving a life sentence for murder, and Gamble was awaiting trial on grand larceny and breaking and entering charges. Strangely enough, their escape didn't become public knowledge until January 1st, when Perry County's newly- elected jailer, Taylor Porter, replaced former jailer Charles Duff. According to Perry County Sheriff John Gross, Duff frequently permitted prisoners to "wander about pretty much as they pleased."

As law enforcement officials were awaiting test results on the items from the FBI, the reward fund that had been established to bring her killer to justice had swelled to $1,635.

Meanwhile, with another grand jury session fast approaching, State Detective Arch Thompson was guarded when asked if any evidence would be presented to it with regards to the Baldridge slaying. "I can't say if it will or if it will not," he said, also refusing to answer questions about the test results on the trousers, pillow, and clothing that were sent to the FBI several weeks ago.

Chapter 16 - An Open Secret

Many throughout Prestonsburg scratched their heads when they heard on Saturday, February 4th, 1950, that the grand jury of Floyd County's Circuit Court had indicted 2 people for Muriel's murder - especially when it was discovered that one of the two men charged in the slaying was Lon S. Moles, an older, well-respected man in the community.

At 60 years old, Moles was a revered member of the Prestonsburg Board of Education, who as a community leader helped oversee the construction of the West Prestonsburg Bridge. He was also a freight agent with the C&O Railroad, where he worked alongside Muriel's father George at the depot just across from the tracks from the Baldridge home. Moles knew Muriel well, as she would often visit the depot after school to see her father or to use the station's telephone.

Moles was married to Elizabeth Moles, who was also a prominent member of Prestonsburg's social scene, most notably serving an active role in the local Floyd County chapter of the Daughters of the American Revolution. Although he was married, some of the employees at the depot believed Moles was smitten with Muriel. His office window was in the front center of the station building, providing him a perfect view into the front yard of the Baldridge home to watch as Muriel and her friends would come and go throughout the day. It was also said that during Muriel's visits to the depot, she would often sit on Moles' desk, talking and laughing with him. It was now being speculated that these encounters may have led to Moles becoming obsessed with the young girl.

Moles was one of several people whom had been questioned over the summer by Detective Arch Thompson, however he had not been considered a suspect until now.

Also indicted was Moles' friend Elbert K. Dotson, better known as "E.K." Dotson, a former restaurant owner and taxicab operator who was from Prestonsburg but was currently living at a family farm in Jackson County, Ohio. Dotson's parents were Mr. and Mrs. E.S. Dotson, whose home was located in the same West Prestonsburg neighborhood where Muriel lived. It was also the nearest home to the murder scene. Interestingly enough, the 45-year old Dotson was one of the five people questioned under "truth serum" earlier in the investigation, but at the time his statements were not considered helpful in providing information about the crime.

Dotson said that he was at his house on the night of the murder, in bed when he heard a dog barking. Dotson went on to add that his mother, who lived with him at the time, turned their hall lights on and asked him if he had "heard somebody holler" outside near the river. Dotson responded to her that he believed it was a dog in the neighborhood.

Dotson's claim that he was in bed at the time of the murder raised eyebrows among some members of the community. "The evening was very humid and and the day was one of the hottest of the year," remarked M.J. Leete, a local pharmacist who worked at the Hughes Drug Store and knew Dotson and Moles well. Leete said that Dotson was known to have been sleeping on the porch "for quite a spell" prior to the evening of the murder. He also said that Dotson had been drinking most of that evening with Lon Moles, and had also been spotted at Coburn's, a local gasoline station, just a few hours after the murder.

Leete also told investigators that he had been issuing prescriptions for a "dope" to Lon Moles fairly regularly over the last year. Leete said that the medication was either called "Sanicol" or "Salicon", and that Moles had been purchasing the medication for several months. He also added that the drug has an intoxicating quality that puts the user in an "'I don't care' mood". He also told investigators that he considered Moles a friend, however he "would not hesitate to tell the truth about anybody."

Although Leete's comments seemed to provide added insight into the case, investigators were not completely convinced of his credibility. "Mr. Leete went on at length with talking about his theories," noted Detective Arch Thompson in his case file, "and continued to talk about the strong possibility of Moles and Dotson teaming up in this killing. Mr. Leete, however, was in a slight state of intoxication and repeated himself continually. It was difficult to terminate this interview."

Meanwhile, Dotson told investigators that he first heard about the murder while watching a crowd of onlookers gather at the crime scene, where he was able

Lon Moles, Freight Agent for the C&O Depot and Member of the Prestonsburg Board of Education. *Courtesy of Barbara (Bolen) Porter*

to view Muriel's body on the riverbank. "Her hair didn't look like her," he said. "Her own people hardly knew her. Her own daddy didn't know her."

In a strange coincidence, Muriel briefly encountered Dotson on the Sunday prior to her murder when Dotson was having car trouble a few miles away from West Prestonsburg at Dewey Dam. Elmer Clifton, a 57 year-old friend of both E.K. Dotson and Lon Moles, shared with investigators that he and his wife saw Dotson's car parked on a road leading up to the Dam, and Dotson was standing beside the vehicle. As Clifton pulled his car closer to Dotson's car, he noticed Muriel Baldridge and two of her friends just a few feet away, walking along the side of the road.

Dotson and his wife exited their vehicle and approached E.K. Dotson. Dotson told Clifton that his car had stalled, and he asked Clifton if he would "push his car up the hill" using Clifton's vehicle. Clifton obliged, but before he and his wife returned to their vehicle, they noticed a man laying in the back seat of Dotson's car.

"I couldn't say positively who it was, but my wife said it was Lon," remarked Clifton. "He was laying down in the car. That is, a man was laying in the car. I couldn't say positively that it was Lon."

Clifton said that Muriel and her friends watched as he pushed Dotson's car to the top of the hill, where

Lon Moles (right) pictured in his office at the C&O Depot in the 1930s. *Courtesy of Mary Burke*

there was another car sitting at the top of the hill. He also commented that Muriel and her friends walked toward the top of the hill, and it appeared that the girls might be looking to get a ride in either Dotson's car or the other car that was parked nearby. In retrospect, Clifton also said that Dotson was acting strangely. "I didn't know what was wrong with him," he said. "He acted like to me he was drinking. I didn't know it before or I wouldn't have pushed him."

Bill Moore and his wife Pearl also witnessed Clifton helping Dotson that day, and he also placed Muriel at the scene. "She was walking up the hill when we saw her," said Moore, although like Clifton, he wasn't sure if she and her friends were hoping to get a ride in either of the vehicles at the top of the hill.

Even though both men hadn't been officially named as suspects in the investigation, there were whispers throughout the community that Moles and Dotson were being targeted as possible suspects in the case. Both Sheriff Epp Lafferty and Deputy Sheriff W.L. Rice admitted that it had recently reached the point of being an "open secret" among those closest to the investigation that Moles and Dotson were being investigated.

A Portrait of the Prestonsburg Chapter of the Daughters of the American Revolution. Elizabeth Moles is in the second row, seated third from right, in a black dress. *Courtesy of the Louisville Courier Journal*

Although it was clear that most of the investigation was focused on Moles and Dotson, Detective Arch Thompson wasn't completely ruling out that there could be other suspects in the case. He questioned a group of friends consisting of Jack Crum, Yancy Horn, Rube Rose, and Sherman Gibson under oath once he learned that the men had been near the bridge on the night of the murder.

The four men, all of whom were local, had been drinking that evening and in the vicinity of the bridge near the time of the murder. Detective Thompson had heard a rumor that in the days leading up to the murder, Rose saw Muriel leaving her home one day in the company of a female classmate and stated "I would give a $5 bill for that." When asked by Thompson if he had also boasted "if I had her out after dark it wouldn't cost me a cent", Rose denied both statements. "That girl was practically raised under my foot," said Rose, saying that anyone claiming to have heard him make those statements had "told a bare face lie."

Detective Thompson was still being secretive about the evidence he and the rest of the investigators had gathered recently, but those close to the proceedings said that "transcribed statements" were the primary evidence that was brought before the grand jury. Shortly after the closed-door session, it was discovered that the transcribed statements were actually sworn statements and affidavits that had been collected by Muriel's brother, Bernard Baldridge, who

George Baldridge (left), seated next to Muriel's brother
Bernard (center) and prosecutor J.A. Runyon (right). *Courtesy
of the Louisville Courier Journal*

Muriel's brother Bernard Baldridge (left), seated alongside her
father George (center) and prosecutor J.A. Runyon (right).
Courtesy of True Detective Magazine

was also the Floyd County conservation officer. Bernard was allowed to read the statements in court, which made for some rare drama during the proceedings.

That afternoon, Moles was served a bench warrant at his home on Goble Street, and was arrested by Deputy Sheriffs Bill Hall, Frank Parsons and W.J. Slone. The arresting officers said that Moles was silent while being taken into custody, and "expressed no surprise at the turn of events." Dotson made the trip back to Prestonsburg with his brother-in-law, Herschell Graham, and his cousin, Elson Kendrick.

Both Moles and Dotson remained in jail while their attorneys devised a strategy. Rather than seek bail for their clients, their attorneys concentrated their efforts on seeking a change of venue for the trial, filing notice with Commonwealth's Attorney John Chris Cornett and County Attorney Woodrow Burchett. For the venue change hearing, Circuit Judge Edward P. Hill vacated the bench, and Chief Justice Porter Sims was in the process of naming a special judge for the upcoming hearing.

Attorneys for Moles and Dotson, both of whom had pled "not guilty" in their first court appearance, knew that a venue change might be the only hope that their clients had for a fair trial. With the hearing just days away, The Floyd County Times eloquently summarized the investigation, calling it "probably the most bizarre and confusing in the annuals of Eastern Kentucky crime", as it had already seen "three confessions of guilt, all of which had later been repudiated and the confessors released and lost sight of at least temporarily."

Overall, the news of the indictment against Moles and Dotson created somewhat of a quiet stir in Prestonsburg; it was considered a "sensation", but nothing more. There was a sense in the community that an "outward show of excitement" might somehow jinx the proceedings, or create enough of a distraction to taint the results of the upcoming trial.

Chapter 17 - The Waiting Game

On Tuesday, February 14th, the legal team for Moles and Dotson received good news as the venue change was granted. Although a trial date was not yet set, it was announced by Special Judge Eldred E. Adams that the trial would take place in neighboring Pikeville before the Pike County Circuit Court.

For the hundreds of onlookers that arrived at the courthouse, it was a rather anti-climactic morning. They "saw little and heard less," as there was little spoken by the attorneys and nothing spoken by Moles or Dotson. Instead, petitions were filed and the proceedings were handled quickly.

The petitions were filed by attorneys W.A. Daugherty and Edward L. Allen, who were representing Moles. Daugherty had a reputation of being the best defense attorney in eastern Kentucky. He was expensive, but rarely lost a case in a court of law. It was considered quite a coup by Moles that he secured Daugherty's services, however public sentiment was that Moles would probably be convicted and sentenced to death anyway. Dotson was represented by attorney Grover C. Allen, who hailed from nearby Jackson, Kentucky, and his law partner from his Jackson, Kentucky law firm of Allen and Williams was also on hand to provide counsel for Dotson. Commonwealth Attorney John Chris Cornett received assistance from County Attorney Woodrow Burchett, as well as assistance from H.R. Burke.

The petitions for both men were identical, with each citing that "the popularity, wide acquaintanceship and relationship of Muriel Baldridge and her parents in this county has aroused such strong and dangerous public opinion against the defendant that it would be impossible to get jurors in Floyd County who would give a fair and impartial trial."

"There is now in and around the courthouse," the petition added, "and in fact, throughout the county an atmosphere of hatred against him (the defendant) so dense that it is, and can be readily observed by visitors, that jurors will be affected thereby and intimidated."

The statements also added that the presence of a reward fund added a great deal of pressure to their ability to defend the clients, and that several county officers and officials were among the group of citizens that went about hiring private detectives to assist in the case. Finally, the petitions went on to add that each defendant feared mob violence would ensue in the event that a "not guilty" verdict was returned in the trial.

After a brief recess, the afternoon session saw an even larger crowd gather inside and outside of the courthouse. It was estimated that 1,000 people were now inside the courtroom, with more than 900 of them standing. Because of the sheer number of people who were occupying the second-floor courtroom, many who occupied the first-floor offices below expressed concern about a possible collapse of the floor above them. This large crowd however, just like the gathering that witnessed the court's morning session, was moderately disappointed that there was no evidence presented, no testimony, and no additional insights offered into the investigation.

A day later, Sheriff Banner Meade took both men to the Pike County jail, and the day after, on Thursday, February 16th, Pikeville Circuit Judge E.D. Stephenson set bond for Moles and Dotson at $15,000

Pike County Courthouse, 1950. *Courtesy of the Pike County Historical Society.*

each. As both men were released under bond, Stephenson made his first attempts at scheduling the trial. Despite an overwhelmingly congested court docket in Pikeville, Stephenson was eyeing late March as the best period for a trial date. "We'll just have to make a place for it," he said, and soon thereafter it was decided that March 27th would be the date.

Chapter 18 - A Date With Destiny

As jury selection began in the Moles/Dotson trial, the feeling was in the air that Muriel's murderer, or murderers, had finally been brought to justice, and that justice would soon be brought to Muriel. Even though no evidence connecting Moles or Dotson had been made public, it was generally felt throughout Prestonsburg that one or both of the men were most likely guilty of the crime - or the grand jury would not have indicted them.

The days leading up to the trial saw legal victories for the state of Kentucky, as the attorneys for Moles and Dotson filed three desperate motions in Pike Circuit Court. The first motion was to have the indictment thrown out altogether, which was quickly denied. The second was to require the Commonwealth "to produce all papers, writings, and documents produced by Bernard Baldridge and read by him to the Floyd grand jury at its January term." This motion was also denied. The third motion asked that the Commonwealth be required "to reveal the names of all witnesses who appeared before the grand jury and who are expected to testify in the trial at Pikeville." Judge Stephenson also denied this motion, however he did direct that the names of all of the witnesses who produced evidence during the grand jury investigation be written on the indictment.

Bernard Baldridge was questioned just after the motions were filed, and he was asked to supply the names of the people who had sworn affidavits in the statements that he provided to the Floyd County grand jury. He was able to provide most of those names to the court officials in Pike County. The stenographer who worked during the January grand jury proceedings, Miss Nora Jane Parker, was also questioned. Miss Parker, who also worked in the office of County Attorney Woodrow Burchett, said that she didn't recall the context or details of the various papers, including Bernard Baldridge's sworn statements, that were presented as evidence during those hearings.

As March 27th arrived and the trial was set to begin, attorneys for Moles and Dotson requested, and received, a continuance. The continuance was granted when the attorneys unveiled an affidavit signed by both defendants, stating that Olen Collins, the 15-year old carnival worker that had initially identified William "Bill" Gamble as Muriel's killer, would again offer his account of Gamble being the killer if called as a witness in the trial. The affidavit also stated that a summons had been issued for Collins in his home county of Magoffin, but that the sheriff there had not been able to execute it because Collins was currently residing in Breathitt County. The defense insisted that they "can and will" produce Collins in the trial, which concerned the prosecution team.

Some in Prestonsburg and Pikeville were confused to whether the continuance was requested by the Commonwealth or by the defense. "The defense had it continued", said Commonwealth's Attorney J.A. Runyon. "They filed written affidavits for a continuance. I did not make a motion for the trial to be continued."

The defense countered that it was actually the court who wanted the continuance. "The affidavit was filed stating Collins had implicated Gamble and would do so again if present as a witness," shared a member of the defense team. "The Commonwealth refused to admit that Collins would so testify, and the court had to continue the case."

The new trial date was set: it was May 15th, and everyone was eager for both resolution and closure.

Chapter 19 - Close at Hand

Just days away from the trial, there was news that William "Bill" Gamble, the former carnival worker who had been considered the primary suspect in the slaying for most of the previous summer, had been found. He was arrested in the Black Hawk Hollow section of Perry County, Kentucky, where he was wanted for jail breaking. He told authorities that he had recently married, and he confessed that his jail escape in Hazard where he had been confined was made by taxicab.

By Wednesday, May 10th, it was announced that both Gamble and Collins were to be reunited in a Pike County jail, as both men on the witness list for the Moles/Dotson trial coming up the next week. Gamble was currently in jail in Hazard, and Collins had just been released from jail in neighboring Salyersville, Kentucky, returning to his home in Duco in Magoffin County. While some doubted that Collins would be held in custody at all during the trial, no one doubted that the trial would be "one of the most interesting in Eastern Kentucky legal history."

The trial began on Monday, May 15th, and although indicted together, it was decided that the men would be tried separately. Lon S. Moles, the venerable, school board member that had also been a co-worker of Muriel's father George at the C&O Railroad depot station, was tried first.

E.K. Dotson (left) watches the Moles trial in Pikeville with his parents, Mr. and Mrs. E.S. Dotson. *Courtesy of the Louisville Courier Journal*

The prosecutors also stated that they would attempt to prove that "a man answering Moles' description got out of a car, similar to his, near the bridge a short time before Muriel's death screams were heard." They also had a witness who would be testifying that they saw scratches on Moles' arms shortly after the slaying.

The first two days of the trial were devoted to jury selection, as 103 men and women were brought before the court. The most poignant question of jury selection came when Commonwealth Attorney J.A. Runyon would ask each potential juror if, given sufficient evidence of guilt, they could inflict the death penalty. By Wednesday morning, a jury of 10 men and 2 women was in place, and it was now time to introduce the long-awaited evidence in the case.

At 1 p.m. on Wednesday, Muriel's father, George Baldridge, became the first person to testify in the case. With a booming voice, George testified that Muriel left home on the night of Monday, June 27th, with some of her girlfriends, and that she had told him that they would be attending a ball game that night. She also mentioned that there was a carnival in town, and that she and her girlfriends might stop by there as well. He said that he was eating breakfast the next morning when some girls came to his porch at 6:30 a.m., telling him that there was a dead girl nearby on the riverbank and they believed it was Muriel.

After rushing to the riverbank, he said that he saw Muriel's body lying motionless there, wearing a blue sun dress. Her head was severely wounded, and there was blood in her blonde hair. He also added that her body had apparently been dragged about 75 feet from the direction of the bridge.

George went on to say that his home is roughly 100 feet from the railroad depot station where Moles had his office. He also said that Muriel went over to the station frequently to use the telephone there.

The next witness was Green Haywood, a Prestonsburg man who said that he accompanied Moles and E.K. Dotson to a bootlegger's home the day after the slaying. Haywood, who also happened to be the father-in-law of Muriel's brother Dexter Baldridge, said that the primary reason for the trip to the bootlegger's house was because Moles wanted "to find out who sold a certain brand of whiskey." He said that Moles was curious about that information, because an empty whiskey bottle bearing that brand name had been found under the bridge by investigators, not far from Muriel's body.

After purchasing whiskey there, Haywood testified that Moles parked the car on a side street near Highland Avenue. "He reached down under him and got a bottle of Four Roses out and I would say it was approximately one-half full of whiskey," said Haywood. "He reached it to me and I told him I hadn't been drinking any in quite a while, and he said 'I am sorry.' He handed it to E.K. E.K. took a drink with him."

Haywood also added that Moles said "I'm going to get drunk. This thing is killing me. This poor little girl never will sit on my desk and joke and laugh with me anymore."

According to Haywood, Moles drove the men rather recklessly down the highway. As they neared the Woodland Inn, Moles sped up and passed some trailers loaded with mining cars, scaring both men. "I thought that we were going to get killed," said Haywood. "E.K. even ducked down under the windshield.

Haywood also mentioned that for several weeks after the murder, Moles would ask him about the case. "Approximately every morning that I would go to Jack Bingham's restaurant, Lon would drop in there and he will ask me 'have you heard any news concerning the Baldridge case?'"

Shortly after Green Haywood's testimony, the bootlegger, Clyde M. Godsey, testified about the evening in question. Godsey said Moles came to his home twice on the morning after the murder, at midnight and at 4 a.m. During the first visit at midnight, Moles purchased whiskey from Godsey with a $20 bill but said, "Don't turn the light on." The bootlegger's wife, Julia May Godsey, also testified during the trial, saying that she couldn't see how to make change for the $20 bill in the dark, so she turned on the light. After turning the light on, she saw bloodstains on the front of Moles' shirt. When asked how much blood she saw on the shirt, she replied "There was a right smart amount."

R.L. Shepherd, a teacher at Prestonsburg High School who testified at the Moles trial. *Courtesy of Barbara (Bolen) Porter*

"When he was there the first time, he only had on a little summer shirt," she continued. "Just a little thin, short-sleeved shirt - yellow. That is how it come to show up on his clothes."

The Godseys said that during Mole's return visit at 4 a.m., he had changed clothing and was wearing a different shirt. "I noticed he had on a gray shirt," said Mrs. Godsey, "something like these policemen wear, with long sleeves in it." She also said that during this visit Moles bought a pint of whiskey, a brand known as Four Roses whiskey, and asked him if anyone else had bought that brand recently besides himself. After Godsey told him no one else had purchased that brand, Moles spoke again. "Remember," Moles said, "I wasn't here last night."

The Commonwealth also called Elvin H. Goble, a Prestonsburg filling station attendant, to the stand. Goble testified that on the day after Muriel's murder, Moles brought his car to the filling station and hired him to replace the seat covers. Goble distinctly remembers a stain on the back seat cover that, although he couldn't tell what it was or what might have caused it, had showed signs of being washed. Goble also went on to add that after he changed the seat covers, he had a conversation with Moles in which they both differed about the date they were changed. Moles, he said, insisted they had been changed an entire month prior to the murder.

Also called to testify was R.L. "Bob" Shepherd, a teacher at Prestonsburg High School, who claimed that he saw wounds on Moles' left arm the day after the murder. He said that he picked Moles up in his car on the afternoon of June 28th, and he asked Moles about how he incurred the injuries, but received no reply. Following Shepherd was R.C. Dyer, a contractor from Prestonsburg, who said that he saw Moles the day after the murder and that he saw scratches on Mole's arms and face.

Betty Lou Tackett was also called to the stand. Tackett, the young high school girl who was visiting a friend who lived near the bridge on the evening of the murder, spoke of hearing screams that night. She also said that she saw a man walking quickly across the bridge, but that he disappeared behind a bridge pillar when he saw two boys speeding across the bridge on a motorcycle. The prosecutor had Lon Moles stand up in the courtroom, and Tackett was asked if Moles looked like the man she saw that evening. Tackett said that Moles didn't fit the description, and that the man she saw appeared to be larger than the defendant.

The day's final witness was Sybil Mackenzie (Moore), who was one of the girls who was with Muriel on the night she was murdered. She said she began the night by meeting Muriel at the Baldridge home, then going with her to the ball game and the carnival. While walking home, Sybil said that an unknown car pulled up beside them, "almost to a stop," and asked them if the girls needed a ride. After declining the offer, the car drove out of sight. She and another girlfriend who was walking with them left Muriel near a garage that was located about a block from the bridge. This was the last time that she saw Muriel alive.

By day's end, the Commonwealth had called 11 witnesses in all. Pinning its hopes on what it perceived to be strong circumstantial evidence in the case, paired with equally powerful witness testimony, it was clear that the prosecution had its sights set on a death penalty verdict against Moles.

The empty whiskey bottle found at the murder scene was a crucial piece of physical evidence for the prosecution, but it wasn't the only piece of evidence they had. The bloodstained shirt that was found at the scene was believed to have been the shirt Moles was seen wearing at midnight, just 2 hours after the murder. Moles' shoe size also matched the footprints that were found at the scene.

Commonwealth's Attorney J.A. Runyon maintained that the evidence would prove that Moles attended the ball game on the night of the slaying, and that he was drinking, and that may have contributed to his state of mind that evening when he killed Muriel.

Chapter 20 - The Alibi

Moles' legal team was polishing its defense, and also publicizing its intent to prove misconduct on the part of Prestonsburg Police Chief Epp Lafferty. Moles' attorney, W.A. Daugherty, contended that Lafferty had attempted to influence a witness in the trial, offering him "$1,000 and a house" for evidence that would convict Moles.

Daugherty also maintained that the defense would be able to prove that Moles was at home, in bed and asleep, at the time of Muriel's slaying.

Moles' attorney, W.A. Daugherty, also maintained that the prosecution had nothing but circumstantial evidence, and questioned the validity of the evidence that would be presented at trial. In the opening remarks for the defense, Moles' attorney W.A. Daugherty called to attention the reward fund that had been established to capture Muriel's killer, calling it a "slush fund", creating a "scrambled situation." He further added that the fund was a "very dangerous thing that may cause somebody to come here and swear something that is not the truth."

Daugherty further added that Moles, at 60 years of age and plagued with a variety of debilitating health problems, was "physically incapable of dragging that girl down the riverbank and beating her to death."

Daugherty's first witness was none other than Lon Moles, who told his accounts of what occurred that night. Moles stated that he attended a softball game on the night in question, and "retired early" after returning home from the game. He maintained that he didn't leave home until 4am the next morning, when he said that he left for work, heading to the C&O depot station. He said he was unaware of the murder until around 6:30 a.m., when on his way back home for breakfast, he saw a large crowd gathered at the scene.

Daugherty was confident that the sworn statement Moles had given Detective Arch Thompson in the Floyd County Courthouse on July 2, 1949 would show the jury that his client's alibi had been consistent throughout the months since Muriel's murder. Daugherty produced the document, which stated:

"I, Leonedes S. Moles, 60 years of age, born at East Point, Kentucky, February 24, 1889 and residing with my wife Elizabeth Goble Moles at 67 Goble Street in Prestonsburg, Kentucky. I have been employed by the C&O Railroad Company Since 1909. I have been arrested once in Prestonsburg for being drunk.

Last Sunday, June 26, 1949, I worked until 11 a.m. and went home, and remained home the best I can remember. I believe I went to bed at 8:30 or 9 p.m.

and got up at 4 a.m. on Monday. After
getting up I went to the Station at 4 or
4:30 a.m. At 5 a.m. it's been my practice
to go to the residence of J.M. Sauers and
take him to the station, then I go home
and make my wife's breakfast. On
Monday, I left the station at 6 or 6:15 a.m.
I entered my car and drove directly home
arriving at 6:30 a.m. I then made my
wife's breakfast, we both ate, and I
returned to the station at 6:45 or 7 a.m.
I remained at the depot until 11:30 a.m.,
returning home for lunch. I returned to
the depot at 1 p.m., where I remained
until 4:30 or 5 p.m. I then left alone and
went directly home, remaining there until
8:15 p.m., a which time Mrs. Victoria
Arnold and Mrs. Nell Riddle visited my
home. I was in my garden working on my
roses. I then put my car in the garage,
located on First Avenue, at 8:15 p.m. As
I was putting my car away I saw lights
burning at the football field. I drove over
to the field where I met Mr. Harkins and
his wife. From the football field I went
directly home and allowed my car to
remain parked outside near the school yard.
I arrived home at 9 p.m. and did not leave
the house during the night.

I got up Tuesday morning at 4 a.m., shaved, and told my wife I would return and make her breakfast. I left home at 4:15 a.m. and went to the Depot. Mr. Sauers was off duty on this day so I remained here alone until 6 a.m., at which time Mr. Standsbury of Louisa arrived. I left the depot at 6 a.m. I got in my car and attempted to drive across the bridge, but the bridge was blocked. Several cars and about twenty people were on the bridge. I stopped and someone said a dead woman is lying down there. I got out of my car and looked over and I saw Mr. Hicky down there. When I saw Mr. Hicky I told him to keep the people away from under the bridge. I then got into my car and drove away. I only talked to Mr. Hicky.

I went directly home, arriving at 6:30 a.m. I told my wife that there was a dead woman on the other side of the bridge. My wife asked who it was and I said I did not know. After eating breakfast, I left my home at approximately 7 a.m. and drove over the river where a large crowd of people were standing on the bridge. I drove directly to the depot. A rumor was going around that the dead girl was Muriel Baldridge. Mr. Standsbury and

Henry Meadows were standing about.

At this time I drove Baldridge and another girl over to the funeral home. When we returned home the bridge traffic was very heavy. These girls made no remarks about the crime. We arrived at the depot at 8:30 or 9 a.m.

I came back to town shortly later and met Mr. Grey and Mr. Dingus. I told these men about a car that I had seen at approximately 6:20 or 6:25 a.m. This car was coming out of a vacant lot near Joe Harkin's. Their car was a Chevrolet, and there were two men and a woman in it. The woman was in the rear seat wearing a hat, and the driver of the car was wearing a coat. One man was wearing a hat. The woman's hat contained a plume. This woman was about 30 or 35, slightly stout. I got the license number of the car after following the car and passing this car after securing the license number. I returned home, took the two women home, and drove back to town and met the Sheriff. We talked for a while then I took him over and showed him where the car came from and then drove the Sheriff back to his office.

I then met Sturgill; he wanted to go over
the river. I drove him over and Mr.
Sturgill left the car. I turned at the circle
and met Mr. Sturgill again and then took
him back to his office. We arrived at Mr.
Sturgill's home at 10 a.m. I then went to
see Chief of Police Blackburn. I drove
him to the scene of the murder and then
back home. I then went back home for a
few minutes and then returned to the depot
at 1 p.m. and remained there for about an
hour.

As I left the depot, Green Haywood and
E.K. Dotson left the car and started
looking for clues. Haywood found two
zippers and said he was going to turn them
over to the law. We remained here for
twenty minutes, which was about 2 p.m.
We then returned to the depot at 2:20 p.m..
I remained at the depot for about a half
hour, then I left the depot and went and
got some whiskey. I went back home
after buying the whiskey and remained
for a short while. I then went back to the
depot and worked until 5:15 p.m., and then
returned home and ate supper and then
returned to the depot at 6:45 p.m. and
remained there until 7 p.m. I returned
home around 7:30 or 7:45 p.m. I was
driving down Route 23 to Harry

Baldridge's home to purchase some beans
just north of Woodland and a car crowded
me and then someone walked in front of
my car and to keep from hitting him I
turned my car and it landed in a ditch.
Someone took me to my home; I believe
it was two men, but I don't recall anyone
wanting to take me to a doctor. These men
drove by my home but I didn't go into the
house. I asked the men to take me to the
depot, which they did. I don't know what
time we arrived at the depot. These men
drove me to get some whiskey before
taking me to the depot. I went to sleep on
the desk in my office until 7 a.m., then I
called a taxi and went home."

Also called to the stand was Mrs. Lon Moles
and her sister, Mrs. Belva Quisenberry, both of whom
testified that Lon was home that evening. Mrs. Moles
said she distinctly remembered him coming home at
9:30 p.m., as a friend of hers had just left her home and
she was waiting for a radio program that began at 9:30
p.m. to start. Mrs. Moles also said that she was awake
until 3:25 a.m., unable to sleep due to her arthritic
pain, and that Lon was in bed during that entire time.
She said that she vividly recalled walking around their
house to exercise her arthritic ankle and sore hip,
which had been fractured last year. She also said she
heard her husband snoring throughout the evening
before taking some "pain tablets" to help her sleep.

Belva Quisenberry (second from left) and her sister Elizabeth
Moles (second from right), pictured with two unidentified
women. *Courtesy of Jim Goble.*

Mrs. Quisenberry said that she was at their
home until 12:45 a.m., and that she turned off the light
that Lon had left burning after he fell asleep reading.
After leaving the Moles' home, Mrs. Quisenberry said
that she went to her mother's house, who lived nearby.
She was awake all night caring for her mother, who
was sick, and she said she could see Lon's car in the
driveway of their home throughout the night.

Mrs. E.P Arnold, who also had visited Elizabeth
Moles on the night of the murder, was also called to
testify. Mrs. Arnold brought Mrs. Jack Ribble, a friend

of Elizabeth's, during the visit. They arrived at 7:30 p.m., and visited with both Lon and Elizabeth Moles until 9 p.m.

"Lon was there until we got ready to leave," said Mrs. Arnold. "Just a few minutes before we left he told his wife he would go move his car because it was parked in front of the school house lot, or see something about his car. He said he would be right back, and I said 'Oh, Lon, we have stayed here so long.'"

Prestonsburg attorney J.W. Howard, as well as Mrs. Alex H. Spradlin, were also called to the stand. Alex Spradlin, a well-liked teacher at Prestonsburg High School, watched from the courtroom as his wife testified before the packed courtroom. Both Howard and Mrs. Spradlin testified that they saw scratches on Moles during the week prior to the murder.

The defense also called Jack Boyd, one of the two young men who crossed the bridge at 10:25 p.m. that evening. Boyd said he and his friend, Donald Conley, had been told "that Muriel was walking alone on the bridge and (they) went to take her home." Boyd said that he saw a man on the bridge dressed in a two-tone western shirt, and said that the man was definitely not Moles.

Alex Spradlin, teacher at Prestonsburg High School. *Courtesy of Barbara (Bolen) Porter*

Moles' attorney also called John Keenon, Jr. to the stand. Keenon said that on June 27th he saw Muriel crossing the bridge into Prestonsburg with her friend Sybil McKenzie. Keenon was visiting the home of Dora Stephens, a family friend. Around 10:15 p.m., he left the Stephens home and had made his way back across the bridge when he heard "three or four screams."

Keenon claimed that, just after hearing the screaming, he walked back across the bridge and saw two men "in their 30's or 40's" clad in tan work clothing, saying one man was about 6 feet tall and the other man was shorter. He also said he saw a man and a woman sitting on the bridge that evening. "I didn't hear what they were talking about," added Keenon, "I took it that he was drunk and she was persuading him to leave."

Also testifying was Moles' good friend and personal physician, Dr. O.T. Stephens, who told the courtroom he had been treating both Moles and his wife for arthritis and rheumatism for nearly 10 years. He also said that he saw Moles' car parked in his driveway twice that evening, just shortly after 10 p.m.

Banner Burchett also took the stand. Burchett was a local coal miner who said he saw two people in a parked car at the carnival that evening, and he identified them as Olen Collins and William "Bill" Gamble. Neither Collins or Gamble was called to the stand.

The defense was fairly confident that their witnesses had cast enough of a shadow of a doubt with the jury to where they would clear Moles of the charges against him. Their biggest stumble, however, came when they were unable to prove that Chief of Police Epp Lafferty attempted to bribe a witness during the investigation. They called Mr. John George to the stand, who along with his wife had reportedly been offered a bribe from Lafferty.

Dr. O.T. Stephens, Lon and Elizabeth Moles' personal
physician. *Courtesy of Barbara (Bolen) Porter*

Mr. George and his wife lived near the crime scene, as they were renting an apartment in a detached garage building on E.K. Dotson's property. Lafferty believed there was a chance Mr. or Mrs. George knew details about the murder, and if Dotson was involved he felt that they might feel obligated to protect him because they were renting their home from him.

Mr. George said that Lafferty never mentioned Moles' name during their conversation. "There's a thousand dollars involved in it for you if you tell what you know," said Lafferty, according to George, "and if you had to move we will furnish you a house and if you are afraid, the law will protect you."

Mr. George also testified that he heard screaming on the night of the murder, but knew nothing else about the crime. Mrs. George was also called to the stand, saying that she too heard screaming but that she thought it came from a dog.

Another witness, Thelma Collins, said that she had a conversation with Mrs. George on the bridge just a few days after the murder. Collins was discussing Muriel's murder with a friend of hers, Mrs. Shepherd, when they met Mrs. George on the bridge.

"Mrs. George came around Dotson's house and laid her packages down," shared Collins. Mrs. George joined the ladies for the walk, asking them if they had heard any news about the case. She told them that

Lafferty had given her and her husband a letter to read, but she didn't comment about the contents of the letter, only saying that he told her that she "was in danger". According to Collins, Mrs. George remarked that some clothes had been found near the crime scene and that recently some kids in the community had been coming on her property looking for more clothing and other evidence connected to the crime. Collins added that Mrs. George said that "the next kid comes around getting rags - I will fill it full of shot."

Collins also said that Mrs. George was concerned that the clothing that was found near the crime scene was "planted to get my husband into it or E.K.," and that E.K. Dotson's father "was going to put a stop on getting E.K. into it." Collins then told Mrs. George that "you will have to stop the whole county and the whole United States. It's in everybody's mouth except the little girl that was killed."

Chapter 21 - The Decision

On Wednesday, May 24th, both sides of the case had wrapped up their closing arguments, and the fate of Lon S. Moles was now in the jury's hands. The jury had deliberated the night before, and was held overnight after reporting to Judge J. Frank Stewart that they had not yet reached a verdict. But it was now morning, and after just 1 hour and 53 minutes, the jury was ready to announce their verdict. It was "not guilty."

As relieved as Moles was upon hearing the verdict, a short while later E.K. Dotson, Moles' friend who was also being charged with Muriel's murder, was equally relieved. Commonwealth Attorney J.A. Runyon announced that the murder charge against Dotson would be dismissed.

One of the jurors, Marvin Williamson, told the media that the jury would have been able to reach a verdict after just 10 minutes, but that one of the twelve jurors believed Moles was guilty, an opinion that differed from the other eleven jurors.

The Baldridge family was crushed. They emptied out of the courtroom as if the wind had been knocked out of them. They were certain that Moles had either killed Muriel or played a role in her slaying, especially Muriel's father George, who was virtually inconsolable. It was now nearly a year since her death, and her family was still without closure. A guilty verdict wouldn't have brought Muriel back, but at least it would have brought some semblance of justice to her family.

Most people throughout Floyd County believed that the trial was simply a case of the jury giving much more credence to Elizabeth Moles' testimony rather than testimony of Clyde and Julia Godsey. As a society woman, Elizabeth was no doubt embarrassed to have her name, and her husband's reputation, damaged by the trial, and those following the trial who believed that Lon Moles was guilty of murder speculated that she lied for him on the stand in order to salvage her reputation and maintain their standing in the community. It was also no secret that Elizabeth had severe health problems in recent years, and that if her husband was sent to prison or executed for the crime, she would be left to live out the rest of her years alone without anyone to care for her.

Clyde and Julia Godsey proved to be the state's best witnesses against Lon Moles, and although their testimony about their encounters with Moles on the evening of June 27th and morning of June 28th was damning, the fact that they were bootleggers didn't help the prosecution's case. Most felt that the jury questioned the validity of the Godseys' testimony because they were bootleggers, which were looked down upon in the community and frequently in trouble with law enforcement officials. Both Clyde and Julia

Godsey had a minor criminal history, the most recent of which included court appearances in Floyd County recently, having been charged with "selling spirituous, vinous, and malt intoxicating liquors."

A few days after the verdict was announced, law enforcement officials returned Muriel's bloodstained dress and other possessions to her family, with her sister Mary Hilary taking possession of her clothing and other personal effects. Within hours, Muriel's mother Bertha privately burned the belongings that had been returned to the family, in the hopes that it would put an end to any future investigations into her daughter's murder. It was suspected that Lon Moles and E.K. Dotson, the defendant who was released after Moles' acquittal, had the same idea. Within hours of the verdict, the bloodstained shirt and other evidence used in the trial was returned to Moles. That same evening, a few members of the Baldridge family watched from their home as smoke billowed out of the chimney of the home of E.S. Dotson, brother of Moles' friend and co-defendant, E.K. Dotson. The family believed that Moles and Dotson were burning the evidence, ironically just a few hundred feet from Muriel's house and the riverbank where she was found.

Less than a month later, Prestonsburg High School's senior class of 1950 graduated. This was a moment she had been looking forward to with great anticipation, yet sadly she was not there. During the ceremony, held within the warm school's gymnasium, a moment of silence was dedicated to Muriel. Tears were shed again for her as her classmates and their families remembered the bright, charming girl who was taken too soon.

Courtesy of Barbara (Bolen) Porter

A few months later, a young art student in his early 20s named Hugh Winston Stumbo came to Prestonsburg to visit with the Baldridge family. The family knew that Stumbo, described as "short-statured, black-haired and baby-faced," had been dating Muriel in the months leading up to her murder, but during his visit he revealed that he and Muriel were also secretly engaged. He had given her a ring, and they had made plans to marry. Heartbroken, Stumbo left the area and had only just now returned to share the news with her family. During his visit, he brought a drawing of

Muriel that he had sketched from memory, giving it to her parents.

The coming days would not get any easier for George Baldridge. Although Dotson had returned hastily to his family farm in Jackson County, Ohio, Moles had not only remained in Prestonsburg, but he kept his position as a freight agent with the C&O Railroad. It was a tense working relationship, as George firmly believed that Moles had killed his daughter.

The two men didn't speak to each other for the first few weeks after the trial until one afternoon when Moles decided to break the silence. Standing just outside of the depot, Moles was talking with Tom Derossett, an acquaintance who had stopped by the depot that day. Moles saw George walking away from the station next to the railroad tracks, carrying a metal lunch bucket and heading towards his house. Moles shouted "Hey George, I want you to set that car off them tracks," referring to an empty railroad car that needed to be repositioned from the main railroad track to a different track that sat behind the station.

After hearing Moles' orders, George stopped, turned, and began walking back toward Moles and Derossett. There was a purpose in George's eyes - a rage that had been simmering for several days that Moles must have underestimated. As he came up to Moles, George grabbed his arm, hit him over the head with his metal lunch pail, and said "I know you killed my daughter, and don't you ever speak to me again you murdering son of a bitch!" Moles fell back, muttering "George" in an effort to reason with him. The two never spoke again.

For the next two years, Muriel's mother Bertha and the rest of the Baldridges tried to get on with their lives, but Muriel's death had left a scar on the family that couldn't be healed. In January of 1952, George Baldridge died at the age of 59. Although he passed away of a heart attack, the family was sure that he actually died of a broken heart.

Elbert Dotson, father of E.K. Dotson, passed away in November of 1952 at the age of 76. Dotson and most of his family had relocated to Oak Hills, Ohio shortly after the trial.

The following year, in May of 1953, the investigation was rekindled when county detective A.L. Davidson was approached by a Prestonsburg woman about the slaying, claiming her ex-husband was the murderer. Accompanied by Sheriff Banner Meade and City Patrolman Amos Gray, Davidson listened as Ellen Foley recounted a story that she claimed was told to her by her ex-husband, Dewey Osborne, when they were still married. Foley said that on 2 separate occasions Osborn told her that he and one of his friends, Clyde Vaughn, confronted Muriel on the bridge that night and struck her with a ball peen hammer.

According to Foley's affidavit, Vaughn said Osborne had wielded the hammer, but in the second version of the story Vaughn claimed that he had delivered the fatal blows but that Osborne was present. Saying that her conscience had been bothering her over the last 4 years, she told authorities it was time to come clean and tell them what she felt she knew about the murder. Osborne was soon arrested in Henclip, a small community near Paintsville. Vaughn was found and arrested the next day.

One of the primary pieces of evidence in the examining trial was a missing letter that Foley claimed had been written by Vaughn two years ago while Vaughn was a patient at the Walter Reed Hospital in Washington D.C. According to the letter, Vaughn made mention of the Baldridge investigation and telling Foley that it was "preying on his mind". He also asked her to come to the hospital and he share information with her about the slaying. Foley had shown Officer Gray the letter after receiving it, but Gray said that he didn't see Vaughn's signature on the document. More importantly, the letter was now missing.

Over 500 spectators attended the arraignment, and local radio station WPRT was present to broadcast the proceedings. With Judge Henry Stumbo presiding,

Vaughn and Osborne testified that they were visiting Prestonsburg at the time and had both attended the carnival on June 27, 1949, however they were not together. Vaughn said that he didn't find out about the slaying until the following morning when his milkman told him. Osborne told the court that he had gone to the carnival with a friend, T.J. Hendrick, and then spent the night at his brother's home in West Prestonsburg. He also said that on the drive home that evening he saw only cars on the bridge, and that he didn't see any pedestrians.

Foley, who had been married twice to Vaughn, testified that she went to Washington D.C. and spent

the night with Vaughn in an apartment house near the hospital. She said that Vaughn told her that he and Osborne had encountered Muriel Baldridge while they had been walking across the bridge that evening, and that Osborne made a remark to her. Shortly thereafter, Vaughn said that Osborne killed Muriel and then went immediately home. Vaughn said that he was "very nervous and walked the floor the rest of the night" according to the statement.

Foley said that a few months later she and Vaughn were staying at a hotel in Auxier when he decided to discuss the murder again with her. After purchasing and drinking 2 half-pints of whiskey,

Vaughn reportedly told Foley about the details of the murder, only this time he was claiming to be the actual murderer. Vaughn reportedly admitted that he "lost his head", struck Muriel with the hammer, and then told Osborne that "he was just as much into it as he was and that he had better not tell it." The statement went on to add that Vaughn left Osborne on the bridge with Muriel's body, went home, and hid the hammer under the floor at his mother's home. The next morning, Vaughn said he had heard about Muriel's body being found underneath the bridge, so he had assumed that Osborne had placed it there.

Vaughn had been employed by Dave Patton, a building contractor in Prestonsburg, and Foley said that is why Vaughn had been carrying a hammer with

West Prestonsburg during the 1957 flood (the C&O Depot can be seen on the right). *Courtesy of the Floyd County Historical Society*

him that evening. Along with Detective Davidson, Sheriff Banner Meade searched underneath the floors of Vaughn's mother's home but wasn't able to locate the hammer.

Attorney Joe P. Tackett, who represented both Vaughn and Osborne, viciously attacked Foley's character, charging that she had been seen recently on a date with a married man. Bill Little, a local policeman, testified that while investigating a recent traffic accident, she emerged from one of the vehicles extremely intoxicated. One of Clyde Vaughn's nieces, Tommy Vaughn, testified that Foley had a poor reputation in town and was "real bad to drink."

Officer Gray testified that he met with Foley after she had returned from her meeting with Vaughn in Washington D.C., and that he asked her if she had learned any additional information from Vaughn during her trip. Gray said that Foley smiled and told him "no". The charges were dismissed against the two men due to insufficient evidence.

Muriel Baldridge. *Courtesy of Mary Ann James and Emily
James Anderson*

Courtesy of True Detective Magazine

WHO

MURDERED

MURIEL?

by ROBERT BENTON

a**TD**mystery

Courtesy of True Detective Magazine

A year later, Muriel's case again received national recognition when True Detective magazine published a lengthy article about her murder investigation for their January 1954 issue.

In a piece titled "Who Killed Muriel?" author Robert Benton was hopeful that one day the case would be solved:

> "The murder of Muriel Baldridge stands today as much a mystery as it was that bright June morning when her crumpled body was found. It remains as sharply etched now in the memories of all Prestonsburg residents as it was then.
>
> They agreed that it seems incredible that, in so small a community, the guilty man never was discovered. They look at each other from time to time, and they have their own ideas.
>
> They name no names, but they know the burden some guilty conscience bears. They are not, any longer, laboring day and night to turn up the key to unlock the puzzle of Muriel's death, but they know that time is on their side.

A slip of the tongue, a word mumbled in
half-sleep, a guilty brain made careless
by a mug of fiery mountain dew, a
quarrel - something, someday, the
residents of the little city feel certain,
will reveal the story that Muriel
Baldridge's lips were sealed to hide."

- Robert Benton, True Detective
magazine, January 1954

In November of 1954, a man named Ernest
Brackin was arrested in connection with Muriel's
murder in Meridian, Mississippi, nearly 500 miles
from Prestonsburg.

Brackin, a 49 year-old house painter, had been
jailed and questioned recently by local authorities
about the Baldridge case. "We're trying to get enough
information to know whether to bring him up here,"
said Deputy Sheriff W.B. Boyd. Sheriff Gorman
Collins had asked Boyd and the rest of his officers not
to publicly comment on the case.

Although the sheriff's department was tight-
lipped about the investigation, news had been leaked
that Sam Stepp, a 35 year-old former Martin County
man who was now living in Pensacola, Florida, had
recently signed an affidavit saying that Brackin had
told him about committing the murder. Stepp, said the

admission was made while the two were drinking at Brackin's home in Meridian.

Brackin's arrest followed the Stepp's arrest on a minor theft charge, which occurred in Pensacola while Stepp was en route to Miami, Florida. Stepp told authorities that he was traveling to Miami to "spend the winter with the rich people" when officers found a notebook in his wallet that detailed his encounter with Brackin in Meridian, which included Brackin's address and some notes about Brackin's confession to the Baldridge murder.

Sheriff Collins, accompanied by Police Detective Ed Combs and Deputy Sheriff Al Patton, left soon afterward for Pensacola, where they met with Stepp and brought him to the Meridian jail where Brackin was being held. The trio questioned Stepp as well as Brackin, who was described as "an alcoholic of nomadic tendencies, mild-mannered, and friendly." Brackin admitted to being in Paintsville recently, but was unable to place his whereabouts on the night of the murder but believed he was "somewhere up north."

Both Brackin and Stepp were interrogated separately, and Sheriff Collins noted that Brackin seemed to have no resentment towards Stepp for naming him as a suspect in the murder investigation. Collins also said that Meridian police officers told him that when they had arrested Brackin for murder, he asked them if the victim was a girl.

While under intensive questioning, Stepp began to change his account of his evening with Brackin. In some versions, Brackin admitted to being the killer, and in other versions, he did not. Stepp also admitted that he had been following news of the case over the last few years.

Stepp's interrogation took a bizarre turn when he told Sheriff Collins that he knew J. Edgar Hoover, the head of the F.B.I. He also claimed that he was an amateur detective and had been in Washington D.C. recently. Collins was also very impressed with Stepp's memory, as Stepp repeatedly recited the Gettysburg Address, chronologically named all of the Presidents of the United States, and listed the names of the F.B.I. chiefs in almost every major city in the country.

Brackin's interrogation was equally confusing. He maintained that his mother and 16 of his relatives had all been hanged the day before Sheriff Collins arrived. Investigators were beginning to wonder if Brackin was either mentally ill or attempting to appear mentally ill in case he had plans of an insanity defense should the case go to trial.

After just a few days, however, charges were dropped against Brackin and both he and Stepp were released from custody by Meridian Detective A.W. Creel. The investigation continued.

Chapter 22 - The Man From Indiana

1957 was an especially difficult year for Floyd County as a catastrophic flood encompassed Prestonsburg and many other cities in eastern Kentucky. Lives were lost, property was irreparably destroyed, and many throughout Floyd County were left homeless. But by December, there was a break in the 8-year old murder investigation of Muriel Baldridge.

On December 8th, Sheriff Gorman Collins announced that extradition proceedings had been initiated against a man named Minor Caldwell Taylor, who was an inmate at the Indiana State Prison. Taylor, 35, had apparently confessed to the crime, but had also implicated two other men, Paschal Smith and Edward Brown, as well as an unidentified blonde woman, in his statement. He said he killed Muriel with a pipe wrench during "an argument over her other men friends." Taylor also drew diagrams of the murder scene, and identified a picture of Muriel.

Taylor said that on the night of the murder, he had arranged to meet Muriel on the West Prestonsburg bridge near her home. He drove to the bridge with Smith and Brown in an automobile that Brown had recently stolen in Chicago. After arriving at the bridge, he said that Muriel was standing there with a female companion, so he picked them both up and they drove away. A short time later, the car needed a flat

Minor Caldwell Taylor, an Indiana prisoner who confessed to Muriel's murder. *Courtesy of the Modesto Bee, Modesto California*

tire repaired, so Brown pulled over to fix the tire while Taylor and Muriel had an argument. Taylor was upset because "she was running around with another bunch of guys."

The argument continued after everyone returned to the car, and culminated when Taylor, who said he had been drinking, clubbed Muriel "four or five times with a pipe wrench." He said that she "moaned several times" before becoming unconscious, and that he and Smith took her body down the riverbank, placing it in the bushes near the water. He said that they then drove to a nearby lumber yard where they let Muriel's companion out of the car.

After leaving town in the stolen vehicle, the men drove to Middlesboro, Kentucky, dropping Smith off and continuing to Floyd's Creek, Kentucky. Once in Floyd's Creek, the two men burned Taylor's clothing and drove south, abandoning the vehicle in Augusta, Georgia. The two men then separated, with Brown returning to Chicago and Taylor venturing to Louisville, where Taylor was soon arrested on the government check theft charge. A week later, Taylor revised his confession and stated that he had acted alone entirely, saying that he hadn't been traveling with the 2 men and that Muriel did not have a companion with her that evening.

Muriel's sister Dee didn't believe Taylor's confession, especially since no one in their family had heard of him until now. "It's a make-believe confession," she said. "Muriel never knew anyone by that name (Taylor). As far as we're concerned it's just a story thought up. We've heard so many confessions before. We've gone through all of this suffering, and that Taylor's story sounds so fantastic. As close as Muriel was to my mother and father, they surely would have known if he had been seeing Muriel."

Paschal Smith, who had been arrested by State Detective K.L. Cornett, was turned over to Sheriff Collins, but was released after police records were discovered that revealed Smith was serving a prison sentence in Michigan at the time of the murder.

Taylor's confession mirrored Bill Gamble's and Leo Justice's confessions years earlier, with a story involving Muriel being taken from the bridge in a car. And like the previous confessions, it was also quickly repudiated. After taking a lie detector test administered at the prison, he admitted that he confessed to the murder because he felt he was being mistreated at the Michigan City prison and that he "would rather serve life in Kentucky than serve a year here."

Under questioning, Taylor admitted that "Edward Brown" actually didn't exist - it was actually an alias that Taylor used on occasion. He went on to admit that the blonde girl in his story didn't exist either, saying that she was only a picture that he had seen in the newspaper. It was also speculated by law enforcement officials that Taylor had read the True Detective magazine that profiled Muriel's murder investigation, as the publication had been readily accessible at his prison.

Sheriff Collins, who had been working on Muriel's case for the last 4 years, believed that Taylor knew more about the murder "than he could have learned merely by being in the community at the time." He was holding out hope that Taylor would be extradited to Kentucky for further questioning. The Kentucky State Police said that they would continue to look into Taylor's involvement in the murder, however it was becoming more apparent that the case would remain open. "We are certainly not in a position at this time to say whether or not Taylor is implicated in this case," said Paul Smith, the director of the Kentucky State Police. "However, we are continuing our investigation."

Chapter 23 - Reopened

1957 came to a close, and it was now appearing as if Muriel's case may never be solved. A few weeks later, Floyd County endured even more heartbreak as a school bus carrying 48 students to school plummeted into the Big Sandy River, killing 26 of the children, as well as their driver. The tragedy, which occurred on the morning of February 28, 1958, shook the community to its very foundation. Coincidentally, Donald "Dootney" Horn, the young man who had garnered publicity during the early days of the Baldridge investigation when he was extradited from Texas, was front and center in the bus accident investigation.

Horn, who owned a towing and salvage business at the time, was driving a wrecker that was attempting to remove an abandoned vehicle on Route 23 when the school bus swerved to miss his tow truck and drove off the highway and into the river. Ironically, the stranded vehicle that Horn was attempting to recover belonged to Banner Burchett, a local coal miner who had testified on behalf of Lon Moles in the Baldridge trial in 1950.

Former Chief of Police Epp Lafferty died in 1961 at the age of 71, and just a few years later, in 1968, Muriel's mother Bertha passed away. With Bertha's death, it was becoming apparent that time was beginning to take its toll on many of the people involved in Muriel's life, as well as those who were forever tied to her horrible death.

A year later, Bernard Baldridge, Muriel's brother that was instrumental in bringing Moles and Dotson to trial, passed away in 1969.

In October of 1973, Lon Moles died, and his wife Elizabeth passed away just a short time later, in February of 1976. Both had remained in Prestonsburg, with Lon confining himself to his home most days, living the life of a hermit because of the years of speculation that he was the murderer.

In 1974, E.K. Dotson, who was charged with Muriel's murder along with his friend Lon Moles in 1950, died in Jackson County, Ohio. Immediately after his death, a rumor began spreading throughout Prestonsburg that he had recently become a born-again Christian, which led him to confess to Muriel's murder on his deathbed, further fueling speculation that he was Muriel's killer.

The years had passed, 33 years to be exact, when Prestonsburg Police Detective David Caudill decided to reopen the Muriel Baldridge case. In May of 1982, Detective Caudill formally charged a 48 year-old Ohio man, Frederick Slone, with Muriel's murder, "based on a confession Slone made and upon the investigation we have conducted".

The C&O Depot in the 1970s, shortly before it was
demolished. *Courtesy of the Floyd County Historical Society*

Slone, a long-time patient at the Toledo Mental Health Center, confessed to the killing to staff members at the facility, who in turn contacted Toledo police. Toledo Detective Arthur Marx then contacted authorities in Prestonsburg, and after a brief investigation, Caudill had Slone extradited from Toledo to Prestonsburg for a preliminary hearing.

"At this point," noted Floyd County attorney Arnold Turner, "all that really is in existence is an individual with a history of mental problems who professes to be the killer. We're operating with a lot of skepticism and caution," he added. "Of course, when someone walks in and says he did it, we have to check it out."

Detective Caudill had long been fascinated by the investigation. "It's a very touchy situation," Caudill said, "even though it's 33 years old, the case still carries a lot of weight." As a longtime resident of Floyd County, he felt very close to the investigation, and had a personal desire to bring Muriel's killer to justice. During questioning, he found Slone's account of many of the details of the case to be vague, but overall he was "consistent with his story."

Some factors in the case were working against Caudill, however. Slone, originally a native of nearby David, Kentucky, would have only been 14 years old at the time of the slaying. Some of his family

The West Prestonsburg Bridge in 2011 (view from the
Prestonsburg side of the Big Sandy River).

The former site of the C&O Railroad Depot in 2011.

members came forward and said that he and his family had moved to Indiana prior to the murder.

As Slone was incarcerated awaiting his hearing, public interest throughout the region in the case began to grow. Lawrence Branham, a Pike County man who investigated the murder for Commonwealth Attorney J.A. Runyon, was interviewed about the case. Reflecting back on his time investigating the case, Branham said that he believed the killing was probably unintentional. Interestingly enough, he contradicted several earlier reports about the investigation, saying that the crime scene showed no signs of a struggle during the attack, and that Muriel's body had been laid to rest near the riverbank and not dragged down the riverbank as previous reports had suggested. He again contradicted previous information by saying that even though it had been raining most of the night, Muriel's clothing was not extremely wet - again suggesting that she was probably killed elsewhere and then carried down to the riverbank and placed near the water's edge.

Citing insufficient evidence, and the fact that the Baldridge family declined to participate in bringing Slone before a grand jury, Slone was eventually released and the case was again cold.

In 1991, Caudill was interviewed again about the Baldridge case after he left the police department. "It's still the most talked about murder in several counties," he said. "It's like a folklore. People teach it to their children." He went on to add that many people reacted negatively toward him re-opening the investigation in 1982, and that he also received a handful of death threats. "People said to let it go," he shared, "to let her rest."

Chapter 24 - A Mystery for the Ages

Many more members of Muriel's family were lost in the years that followed. Her brother Dexter passed away in 1985, and her brother J.R. passed away in 1998. Her sister "Med" moved to Ohio and died quietly in her home, and her sister "Dee" died in 2009. As of 2011, her sister Irene remains Muriel's last surviving sibling and closest relative.

During the writing of this book, I encountered many people who were at least somewhat familiar with her story, most of whom were intrigued by the mysterious circumstances surrounding her death and the investigation that followed. It seemed that hardly a day went by when I wasn't asked "Who do you think killed Muriel Baldridge?"

After all of my research, it has become very clear that the answer to that question will always remain unclear. Most Floyd County residents today still believe that Lon Moles was the killer, and that his reputation in the community helped absolve him of being punished for the crime. To this day, it is steadfastly believed by Muriel's family that Moles or his friend, E.K. Dotson, committed the murder.

If the crime had happened today, the chances of solving the murder would be vastly increased. With the advent of DNA testing, many of the items found at the crime scene, such as the lead pipe, the bloodstained clothing, and liquor bottle would likely yield results that could provide invaluable assistance to investigators. Sadly, virtually every piece of physical evidence in Muriel's case was either lost or destroyed, making the chances of identifying her killer next to impossible.

While researching her case, I was hopeful that there might be some existing crime scene photographs that were taken at the time of her murder. I found some case notes from October of 1949 indicating that "existing negatives" were on hand at Strahan's Studio in Prestonsburg. Sadly, a massive fire in February of 1971 at the studio destroyed most of the photographs and negatives that were in their archives.

Muriel's murder investigation remains open in Floyd County, however it is a "cold case" and is likely never to be revisited or reopened by police investigators. Despite the public's fascination with the case, the slaying took place over 60 years ago, and virtually everyone who had been considered a suspect in the case has died. Even if investigators solved the mystery, chances are the killer would escape punishment since he is likely already dead. At the very least, one can at least hold out hope that the truth will one day be revealed, and in May of 2011, those hopes were given new life.

During the course of my own investigation, I received a call from a gentleman in Corbin, Kentucky, who had seen a newspaper article about this project. He told me that he was related to both R.L. "Bob" Shepherd, the teacher who testified in the Moles trial, as well as Olen Collins, the 15 year-old carnival worker that claimed to have witnessed William Gamble kill Muriel. The caller's name was Gene Shepherd, and he told me that R.L. Shepherd had passed away many years ago, but he was fairly certain that his cousin, Olen Collins, was still alive and living somewhere in Kentucky.

Gene told me that even though he hadn't spoken to him in several years, his cousin was originally from Magoffin County, Kentucky, and would currently be 77 years old. Gene volunteered to get Olen's current contact information from their mutual family members and call him, and then Gene promised he would call me back to tell me what he found out.

After getting off the phone with Gene, I was ecstatic - I couldn't believe that I might actually soon be speaking with Olen Collins. I had so many questions that I wanted to ask him, hoping that he could finally shed some light on what really happened on the evening that Muriel was murdered.

A short time later, Gene called me back and said that he had telephoned Olen, and spoke with him briefly. Gene said that he told Olen that I was working on a project about the Baldridge murder, and he asked him if he was "the same Olen Collins" that figured prominently during the investigation. Gene said that Olen gruffly told him "no", and that we "had the wrong person." Gene went on to share with me that he was convinced that his cousin was indeed "the right person."

Later that summer, in August of 2011, I released the first edition of this book, and was excited to see Muriel's case again gaining attention throughout the state. The case was profiled by reporter Adam Baker on WLEX Channel 18 news in Lexington, Kentucky, as well as across the state in various radio shows and newspaper articles. Along the way I met several of Muriel's relatives, including Kara Murphy (Cosby) and her sister Kirsten Murphy, as well their mother, Connie Clark Murphy. Connie, whose mother is Muriel's sister Irene, donated a large box of documents about Muriel's case to me in the spring of 2012, in the hopes that they might help shed more light on the case.

A few weeks later, in May of 2012, I was very surprised to hear from Kesha Collins, the daughter of Olen Collins. I told her that her father had previously denied being "the same Olen Collins" from my conversations last summer with Gene Shepherd, but she said that her father was definitely the same man who had been such a key figure in the investigation many years ago. Kesha said that she had recently been speaking to her father about coming forward and sharing his story with me, and although he was initially reluctant to do so, she was hopeful that he would change his mind.

I was excited to say the least; to think that after 63 years, a man who figured so prominently in Muriel's murder investigation was still alive, and that he might actually hold the keys to solving this case. I knew that speaking with him would probably be the last chance we would ever have of finding out the identity of Muriel's killer. It could also very well be the last chance to provide answers, and more importantly closure, to Muriel's family.

Kesha encouraged me to speak with her mother Daisy, who is Olen's wife, hoping that talking with Daisy would be the best route in order to get Olen to share his story. I called Daisy and spoke with her a handful of times in August of 2012 to see if Olen would allow me to interview him. She said that he wasn't ready to talk yet, but that I could check back with her periodically in case he changed his mind.

In my last conversation with Daisy, she told me that Olen was "ready to talk" to me about the night of the murder, however she said that "it's gonna cost." I was taken off guard a bit, as I didn't expect that Olen would be interested in charging a fee for the interview, especially in light of the fact that his story could bring closure to Muriel's family and help solve a case that has been a mystery to so many people for so long.

Although it is my policy that I never pay for interviews, I made an offer to Daisy and it was rejected. I told her that if Olen ever decides to change his mind and accept the offer, I would definitely be interested in interviewing him about the case. I was also curious to hear what Olen would say to me should an interview happen in the future, so I asked Daisy if he would confirm everything that he had initially said in his 1949 testimony. She assured me that he would not only confirm his testimony, but that he had a lot of other information that would "turn this case on its ear."

Despite my failure to interview Olen, I was intrigued by the fact that Daisy said he would confirm his earliest account of witnessing Muriel's murder during the interview. Since Olen's testimony included witnessing fellow carnival employee William Gamble kill Muriel, I wondered if the interview would lead to the case being reopened. If so, then the first order of business would be determining the whereabouts of William Gamble, who would be 87 years old if he is still alive. In my research with this book, I have been unable to find out whatever happened to William Gamble. I wonder if Olen Collins knows, and if that might be part of the reason why he is so reluctant to speak with me about this case.

If we are left to assume that Muriel's killer was one of the men who were considered viable suspects in the investigation, the most logical candidates would be Moles, Dotson, and former carnival worker William

Lon Moles (top), pictured with 2 unidentified boys in 1933.
Courtesy of Jim Goble

Gamble. Although the court of public opinion still holds Lon Moles, and to a lesser degree, E.K. Dotson, accountable for Muriel's murder, I feel that we should give just as much credence to the belief that Gamble might actually be the killer. Whereas the circumstantial evidence against Moles and Dotson was very strong, both were older men without a criminal history. On the other hand, Gamble had a very extensive criminal record, and had recently fled Virginia as a suspect in the kidnapping, and possible murder, of a young couple. And although it was later repudiated, he confessed to the crime.

In the summer of 2012, I had the privilege of discussing the case with Detective Robert Sarrantonio of the Lexington, Kentucky Division of Police. Detective Sarrantonio is the coordinator for Bluegrass Crime Stoppers, and along with Detective Chris Schoonover, a fellow officer who is in charge of Lexington's cold case unit, read my book and offered several insights into Muriel's murder and its investigation. Together, they have over 40 years of law enforcement experience, and it was interesting to hear their investigative perspective about the case.

"In 1949, law enforcement did not have the technology to assist with murder investigations as we do today," says Detective Sarrantonio. "But we feel there were still critical issues overlooked by investigators even in that era of law enforcement that hurt the possibility of solving this case. First, on the morning that Muriel was found, investigators did not secure the crime scene to prevent contamination. Despite the fact that DNA evidence was unheard of at the time, evidence of shoe and fingerprints were available, but that evidence was compromised when investigators allowed people from the community to come into the area where Muriel laid."

"The most important mistake by law enforcement was the collection of evidence. The whiskey bottle and the metal pipe that were found at the scene should have been collected and fingerprinted. The disappearance of several pieces of evidence is another concern. The other question that comes to us concerns her purse, which most young girls carry. Did she have a purse, and was there an attempt to locate it?"

"The biggest issue is returning key pieces of evidence back to the victim's family and the suspects. When the case is still open, regardless of an unsuccessful prosecution, custody of the evidence should remain with law enforcement. If we had some of that bloody clothing, whiskey bottle, or pipe today, we could run tests to determine or eliminate suspects. Law enforcement, even from that era, should have known to keep evidence involving unsolved crimes, especially murder."

"We are also curious to know if there are any other photographs of the crime scene. It appears the crime scene photographs are limited, and notably absent are photos at the scene before Muriel's body had been removed. Since it was such a high-profile case for that area, photographs of the onlookers should have been taken at the scene as well."

"There was a lot of pressure on the investigators to solve this case and we are aware of that. Even in today's world of social media and 24-hour news networks, law enforcement is under a microscope and is under pressure to solve cases quickly. It is our opinion that there were too many investigators involved in this case. The politics and dynamics of a small, rural town worked against the detectives in this situation because of everyone wanting to be involved."

"The worst form of evidence to build a case on is witness or suspect statements. The investigators relied too heavily on the statements of career criminals, and their tunnel vision directed towards Moles and Dotson eventually hurt them in the trial. For example, all of the suspects were male, but if you let the evidence from the scene guide you it will show you that the suspect could be either male or female. The lack of corroboration of the statements came back to haunt them in court, and at best, the prosecutors had a weak circumstantial case."

"In today's era, we are afforded great tools to assist us in the solving of murders. The use of DNA would have helped tremendously in a case like this.

The securing of a crime scene is crucial in any investigation, especially involving one that had so many pieces of physical evidence. We can also take digital photographs of the crime scene, as well as aerial photographs taken from a helicopter. Schematic drawings of the crime scene help a great deal in court by presenting a visual picture to the jury. We find jurors like 'hands on' type of evidence, such as diagrams and photographs."

"Based entirely on reading the book and not having any knowledge of the actual case file regarding the murder and its investigation, we do have a theory about the crime. After Muriel left her friends to walk across the bridge to go home, none of her friends stated that they heard or saw anyone on the bridge when they walked away. With this in mind, we feel that Muriel met someone she knew and felt comfortable enough with while walking across the bridge. Next, she walked with this person down to the area where she was murdered. There were no reports of blood spatter on the bridge, nor any evidence of struggle from the bridge to the riverbank, such as damage to the brush line. Also, the reports of her screams being heard were in the area of the crime scene and not the bridge."

"The fact that she was dragged leads us to believe that one person was involved since she appeared to be small in stature. We also consider the whiskey bottle to be a key piece of evidence. We believe she walked to the area with a friend and possibly they were drinking. Muriel's torn dress suggests that his person may have made sexual advances toward her, which Muriel rejected, angering the suspect and leading him to assault Muriel. After realizing what he had done, he attempted to drag her body into the river but was unsuccessful, either because he was scared off or because he didn't have the strength to pull her into the river."

"It is our opinion that none of the suspects mentioned in the book committed the murder. One reason to support that is a large percentage of people who commit murders tend to have the natural reaction to distance themselves from their crime scenes. For example, Lon Moles worked next to the bridge, and E.K. Dotson lived next to the bridge. If either had committed the crime, they would have attempted to move Muriel's body as far away from the area as possible. If it were one of the carnival employees, we believe that they would have taken her by car and that her body would have never been found."

"We believe that Muriel was close to her murderer and trusted this person greatly. There could also have been a relationship between the two which led to her death. Being that Muriel was a young, attractive, popular teenager, envy and jealousy could have been motives for a female. Most murders are committed by a person that the victim knows."

Prestonsburg has changed over the years, and progress has been kind to the community. But even though the city has grown in size and population, it has retained its small town charm.

The Irene Cole Memorial Baptist Church is still there, as are many of the stores and shops that dot the downtown landscape. The old courthouse is gone, however, replaced by a modern replica that serves as a tribute to the architecture of its predecessor. The old high school is also gone, with the new Prestonsburg High school having been built on the exact site where the infamous carnival was held in 1949.

Today, the West Prestonsburg neighborhood looks quite different, especially the areas that Muriel knew well. The bridge was condemned by the city in 1989, fenced off and closed to the public. Graying and crumbling, it sits silently as the steady waters of the Big Sandy roll underneath its majestic span, serving as a constant reminder of one of the most painful chapters in the community's history.

The depot is gone, having been demolished when the C&O Railroad decided to leave the county, however the railroad tracks remain, occasionally bringing trains rumbling through the neighborhood.

The Baldridge house has also vanished, and so too have most of the memories of the loving home that George and Bertha provided for their children, as only a few of the people who personally knew Muriel and her family remain. But for those who were blessed to meet her or know her, they remember her fondly, and with loving hearts. They remember her as a warm, wonderful young woman who touched everyone who met her during her short time on earth. And for those who didn't know her, one can only hope that this book sheds some light into her life and her story.

Special Thanks to:

Lynn and John Preston
Ruth Goble
Sybil MacKenzie
Mary Burke
Debi Manuel
Navajo Austin
Misha Curnette
Ralph Davis
Steve Hensley
Jimmy Derossett
Gail Hall
Kait Osborne
Mary Anne James
Emily James Anderson
Cassie Allen
Marge Crisp
Mr. and Mrs. Thomas D. Lafferty
Jack and Connie Parsons
Whitney Parsons
Allen Bolling
Keith Caudill
Scott Hall
Andrew Moore
David Sloan
Jeffrey Scott Holland
Margo Hunt
Toy Reardon
Gene Shepherd
Gordon Belcher

Additional Thanks to:

The Floyd County Times
The Louisville Courier Journal, Louisville, KY
The Pike County Daily News, Pikeville, KY
The Paintsville Herald, Paintsville, KY
The Pittsburgh Post-Gazette, Pittsburgh, PA
The Modesto Bee, Modesto, CA
The Telegraph, Dubuque, IA
WYMT-TV, Hazard, KY
Kentucky State Police, Frankfort, KY
The Prestonsburg Tourism Department, Prestonsburg,
KY
The Floyd County Historical Society, Prestonsburg,
KY
The Mountain Arts Center, Prestonsburg, KY
The Jenny Wiley State Lodge, Prestonsburg, KY
City Florist, Prestonsburg, KY
The Big Sandy Community and Technical College,
Prestonsburg, KY

About the Author

Michael Crisp is a native of Georgetown, Kentucky, and has spent over 20 years in the entertainment business. After graduating from Georgetown College, Michael toured many parts of the country as a singer, guitarist, disc jockey and comedian. In recent years, he became an award-winning filmmaker, having directed and produced *The Very Worst Thing*, a documentary film that revisits the 1958 Floyd County (Ky.) school bus disaster. The film won the Storyteller Award at the 2010 Redemptive Film Festival in Virginia Beach, Virginia. Michael's other directorial credits include *When Happy Met Froggie, Legendary: When Baseball Came to the Bluegrass, A Cut Above: The Legend of Larry Roberts,* and *The Death of Floyd Collins*.

Michael resides in Georgetown with his son, Conner.